GOD'S PLAN OF REDEMPTION

Mary E. McDonough

LIVING STREAM BOOKS

A Publication of Living Stream Ministry • Anaheim, California 92801

First Edition, October 1999

ISBN 0-7363-0718-4

Published by

Living Stream Ministry
2431 W. La Palma Ave., Anaheim, CA 92801 U.S.A.
P. O. Box 2121, Anaheim, CA 92814 U.S.A.

Printed in the United States of America

99 00 01 02 03 04 / 9 8 7 6 5 4 3 2 1

CONTENTS

THE TRIUNE GOD

UNCREATED LIFE

FIG. 1

THE FIRST ADAM

CREATED LIFE

FIG. 2

THE SINLESS ADAM

SPIRIT

SOUL

BODY

FIG. 3

THE FALLEN ADAM

SPIRIT

SOUL

BODY

FIG. 4

THE GOD-MAN

SOUL
BODY

THE LAST ADAM

FIG. 5

THE SIN BEARER

THE LAMB OF GOD

FIG. 6

RESURRECTION

SOUL
BODY

ALIVE FOR EVERMORE

FIG. 7

IN HIM: LIFE

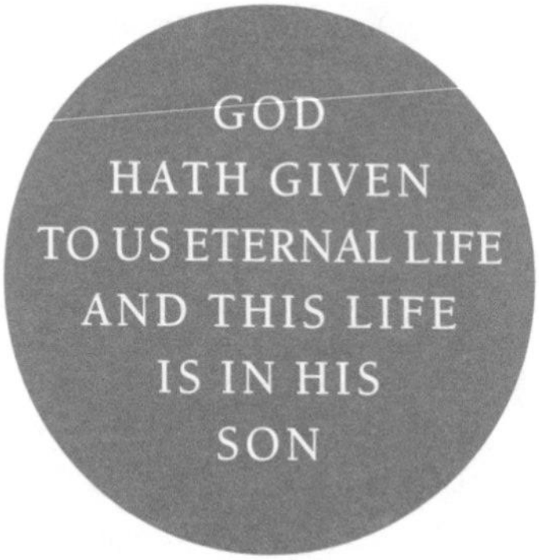

GOD
HATH GIVEN
TO US ETERNAL LIFE
AND THIS LIFE
IS IN HIS
SON

CHRIST OUR LIFE

FIG. 8

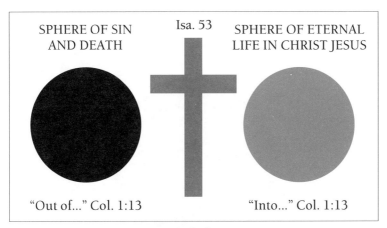

FIG. 9

FIG. 10

TRANSFORMATION

FROM GLORY TO GLORY

FIG. 11

"LIKE HIM...SEE HIM AS HE IS"

MANIFESTATION OF SONS OF GOD

FIG. 12

PREFACE TO THIS EDITION

God's Plan of Redemption is a remarkable study of the believers' full salvation. It mainly unveils (1) the Triune God as the uncreated, eternal life, signified by the tree of life in Genesis 2:9 and Revelation 22:2; (2) the tripartite man created by God with a spirit, soul, and body to be a vessel of the eternal life; and (3) God's eternal plan to dispense Himself as life into man.

This work of dispensing was fully made possible through Christ's redemption, which was carried out by His substitutionary death, attested by His glorious resurrection, and proclaimed in His victorious ascension. This dispensing is now appropriated by the believers in the way of life. It begins from man's spirit at the time of his regeneration, continues in man's soul through the life-long process of transformation, and culminates in his body at the time of his glorious transfiguration. Such a full salvation produces the many sons of God, who are conformed to the image of the first-born Son of God through the divine life-principle. They are built up as the Body of Christ in an organic oneness and prepared as the bride of the Lamb in the divine love, unto the eternal glory of God.

Concerning the charts in this book, Witness Lee said, "To my realization, these charts are the best of their kind in all the publications of Christianity....The charts presented here are very revealing, giving us a clear vision and impressing us with God's plan, His way in His redemption, and the way of life." He referred to Mary McDonough's book as a "marvelous masterpiece" and said, "It is remarkable that we cannot find this book in almost any Christian bookstore in this country." Because of this, we felt that we had to reprint this precious book to make it readily available to all the Lord's children.

This edition retains the original text of the 1920 American edition of Mrs. McDonough's book. No editorial liberties have been taken with the text, other than minimal adjustments to punctuation and typographical style. Additional titles have been added to the charts, according to the British edition of 1922.

We pray that the riches of the divine revelation presented in these pages and the experience disclosed by these truths will become the daily portion of His loving seekers, as our sister wrote, "There's a Man in the glory whose Life is for me....His Life in the Glory, my life must be."

The editors
October 1999

FOREWORD BY THE AUTHOR

The pernicious teaching of evolution in our schools and colleges, and the higher criticism of our modern pulpits, are responsible for the fatal drift from the avowed faith of our forefathers.

This alarming condition calls for new methods of presentation of the truths of God's Written Word.

Experience has demonstrated the wisdom of teaching the fundamentals from the biological standpoint, thereby counteracting in a logical, convincing manner the destructive work of infidel teachers, and saving the young from their subtle snares.

The desirability of presenting these vital truths in a comprehensive manner, with due regard to the unity and correlation of subjects, has also been considered in the preparation of this course of Bible Study; but the treatment of the various subjects does not claim to be exhaustive.

Further study of each subject will repay the Bible student and is strongly advised.

Suggestions in reference to such study will be found throughout this course.

It will be observed throughout these studies, that Eternal Life is presented from the biological standpoint instead of the etymological. While the best authorities agree that *aionios* may be used with reference to the past as well as to the future, yet this word does not clearly reveal the nature of the Life that is bestowed at the instant of regeneration. The term *Uncreated Life* actually defines the Life of God in Christ Jesus, that is shared by the believer. A careful reading of John 1:1 and 1 John 1:1-2 corroborates this statement by declaring Eternal Life to be the Uncreated *Word* who was *with God* the Father, and who *was God*.

Part 1

GOD'S PLAN OF REDEMPTION

The following suggestions to Bible teachers are the result of years of prayerful thinking and careful testing in various Bible classes.

Owing to the fact that comparatively few persons, even in our churches, have plainly perceived the complete cycle of Redemptive Truth, it has seemed wise to group our studies around the Cross of Calvary in such a manner as to clearly reveal GOD'S PLAN OF REDEMPTION.

Under this head we will consider—
First – Those conditions which make Redemption necessary.
Second – God's Plan of Redemption fully executed at Calvary.
Third – The results of Redemption appropriated and manifested.

In starting a Bible Class do not spend time in the endeavor to prove the Bible to be the Word of God. Take it for granted that the persons who have gathered for study believe the Bible to be *God's Written Word*. If there are any present who do not believe this, it is illogical to read to them passages from a book which they do not believe to be infallible to prove its infallibility. And do not argue with them. Simply ask them to study the Book for themselves and then proceed to present its truths in such a manner that the lessons will prove the Bible to be God's Word indeed; even as we prove the truth of a disputed question by a mathematical or chemical demonstration.

The most logical way to read a book is to open to the first page; therefore, without apology, ask your class to read the first five words of Genesis.

GOD – THE CREATOR

"In the beginning God created." Call attention to the fact that God, the Creator, was not created; therefore we may speak of Him as *Uncreated*. Ask the class to think of God, the Creator, in His Uncreated existence before Creation. Lead them to see that He was as perfect, as complete before Creation as after; that His creative acts did not add to His uncreated perfection. Do not hasten over this subject, for the value of all subsequent lessons will depend upon the clearly perceived difference between Uncreated Life and that which is created.

UNCREATED LIFE

Lead the class to see that Uncreated Life has no beginning and no end; that it is self-existent and unchangeable. Ask them to draw or to name some geometrical figure that may symbolize such Life. Doubtless they will suggest the circle. If practicable have some member of the class draw this symbol upon the blackboard or paper. At this point it will be well for the teacher to produce her own symbol, which in the charts used to illustrate this course of study is a piece of white cardboard, fourteen inches in length and eleven inches in width, to which is affixed a large disc of gilt paper with the words "The Triune God" printed at the top of the card and "Uncreated Life," below. (See Fig. 1.)

As the eyes of all are fixed upon the golden disc, which has "no beginning and no end," call for Psalm 90:2 and Psalm 102:27 to be read or repeated.

Now have the entire verse (Gen. 1:1) read. "In the beginning

God created the heaven (or heavens) and the earth," i.e., the universe. Suggest the thought of the impossibility of God's creating the universe without a definite purpose concerning each atom of the same.

Illustrate by the fact that the work of human hands is first carefully planned. Nothing worthwhile is fashioned apart from a plan—a pattern—a formula.

Enlarge upon the thought that God created the universe because He wished it created, and He created it as He wished it to be. (Read Rev. 4:11, last clause.)

ORDER OF CREATION

Call attention to the order of creation. First, heaven and its inhabitants, the angels; then the earth with its various forms of life.

That the Celestial heaven with its inhabitants was created before the earth we may discover as we read Job 38:4-7. God Himself is the Spokesman here. He is talking with His servant Job of His creative power and in exquisite poetry represents Himself as the Master Workman sending forth into space the earthly orb to complete the delicate harmony of the spheres, and over which the "sons of God," i.e., the angels, "shouted for joy." It will be helpful if an article on the music of the spheres is read by the members of the class. The expression "when the morning stars sang together" is not merely a bit of wonderful poetry but it indicates a fact that scientific discovery has brought to light. The chapter on "Scientific Truth of the Word" in Dr. A. T. Pierson's helpful volume, *Many Infallible Proofs,* will be of use in this connection.

How much more satisfactory is this description of a created planet than the theory of "a bit of fire-mist evolving a confused mass of primal elements, which constantly assuming new proportions, finally, after untold ages, appeared as the globe upon which we now live"—and how did the "primal elements" originate?

It is not the purpose of this course of Study to unfold the wonderful scientific truths that are contained in the remainder of this remarkable chapter; but the devout scientific man might refer to sentence after sentence that antedates the discoveries of science by thousands of years: E.g., who would have supposed that verses 22 and 23 had any connection with some of the high explosives of modern warfare; yet devout scientific men now understand the allusion.

ANGELIC LIFE

Let us now turn our attention to the first created beings—the angels. These are unembodied (not disembodied) personal beings— superior to known laws of matter. They may appear in bodily form as many passages of Scripture prove. (See Num. 22:23; 1 Chron. 21:15-16, 18, 20, 27; Acts 12:7-10.) They possess great power and might (2 Pet. 2:11). They "excel in strength" (Psa. 103:20). In 2 Thessalonians 1:7 and the Revelation, we read of "mighty angels." This qualifying adjective would lead us to think that angels vary in rank and authority, and this supposition is borne out by other passages that indicate their rank or order. Thus we read of "principalities, authorities, world-rulers," in Ephesians 6:12 (Rotherham translation).

The names of only two holy angels are given in the Bible— Michael and Gabriel.

The meaning of angel is "messenger," and we see that the holy angels are constantly serving their Creator by going on His errands throughout the universe. Notice that they do not choose the scope of their ministry. They accept the ministrations assigned them without question, as cheerfully going to call a hungry, discouraged servant of God to a meal (1 Kings 19:5) as to utter the transcendent announcement of a Redeemer's birth. The angels are the servants in God's great household. (See Heb. 1:13-14.)

We now approach a subject of great importance, but little understood.

ORIGIN OF SIN

A terrible discord arises in the harmony of the universe. We find the cause of this set forth in Ezekiel 28:12-17, beginning with the last clause of verse 12. The Creator is saying to the wisest, fairest, brightest of the angels, one whom He addresses as "anointed cherub," "Thou wast perfect in all thy ways till iniquity was found in thee"; and He proceeds to pronounce judgment upon him, saying, "Thou hast sinned: therefore I will cast thee as profane out of the mount of God. I will destroy thee, O covering cherub, from the midst of the stones of fire." What was his sin? Let us turn to Isaiah 14:12-15 where God is addressing the same being, calling him by his name Lucifer (son of the morning): "Thou hast said in thine heart, I will ascend into heaven, I will exalt my throne above the stars of God; I will also sit upon the mount of the congregation in the uttermost parts of the north; I will ascend above the heights of the clouds; I will be like the Most High."

Notice the expression "Thou hast said in thine heart." This indicates an attitude not only of mind but of will. It is more than an intellectual process. It is the crystallization of intellectual thinking into an attitude of fixed determination. Five times Lucifer says, "I will," thereby plainly revealing his attitude toward his Creator.

A close study of God's Word seems to indicate that to Lucifer had been given dominion over the earth and its surrounding atmosphere, i.e., the atmospheric heaven. The title "Anointed Cherub" seems to indicate the fact that not only was he a tributary ruler, or prince, but that God had created him to magnify His holiness and exult His Name throughout the universe. The expression, "The workmanship of thy tabrets and thy pipes was prepared in thee in the day that thou wast created," would cause us to believe that he was to lead the great anthem of praise to the Creator throughout the universe.

Notice his expressions very carefully: "I will ascend into heaven," i.e., "heaven itself," the place of God's immediate presence, the "heaven of heavens." Not content with dominion of the lower sphere he would exercise dominion in the Celestial sphere. "I will exalt my throne above the stars of God," points to the fact that he would elevate his throne in the terrestrial heaven, above the starry heaven, even to the Celestial heaven (the "third heaven" of 2 Corinthians 12:2). The words, "I will sit also upon the mount of the congregation, in the uttermost parts of the north," denote the exalted position he intended to occupy—*universal dominion.* "I will ascend above the heights of the clouds," reveals the fact that his seat of dominion was in the atmospheric heaven, and he planned to extend his dominion by invading those regions over which God alone exercised authority and control. "I will be like (or equal to) the Most High," plainly shows us that *equality with his Creator* was his objective. Nay, more than this—he would hurl God from His throne and take His place. No wonder, then, that those solemn words rang through the universe—"Thou hast sinned." Never had those words been uttered before, for this was the origin of sin, and in Lucifer, we behold the first sinner.

We see, then, that the modern teaching concerning sin as being merely a belief of the human mind is erroneous, for sin originated untold ages before the mind of man was created.

SIN DEFINED

We are also enabled to see what sin really is. Contrary to the thought of many who define sin merely as an *act,* we find it to be an *attitude.* Before Lucifer had performed one act of a sinful nature, sin was in his heart. All of the diabolical plans of his corrupted wisdom; all the deceit and subtle, crafty working of his great power, are but manifestations of the sin in his heart when he said, "I will"—*I* instead of God; therefore we may define sin as an *attitude of wilful, deliberate resistance to the authority of God.* Let the members of the class turn to 1 John 3:4 and compare with the Revised

Version which renders "transgression," *lawlessness*. Explain the difference between the two words and show how one might transgress without being lawless; e.g., a foreigner coming to our shores might break some of our laws through ignorance, unintentionally; while another person, with knowledge of our laws, might wilfully, deliberately break them. Lawlessness is deliberate transgression; therefore sin is lawlessness. The manifestations of this lawless attitude are *sins,* or transgressions.

DIFFERENCE BETWEEN "SIN" AND "SINS"

We must not confuse *sin* and *sins*. Sin is the wilful attitude toward God; sins are the wilful acts that are the result of sin. Sin is the tap root; sins are the rootlets. Sin is invisible until manifested in sins. "Sins" is not the plural of sin, but rather the manifestation of sin. Sin is what God sees; sins are what men see. God's estimate of a being is not what he *does* but what he *is*; therefore, *a being who puts self in the place of God is a sinner, no matter how this sin is manifested*. Impress upon the class that sin is a terrible reality. It is a dethronement of God.

Ask the class to read these two remarkable passages, Isaiah 14:12-15 and Ezekiel 28:12-19, carefully many times. As they look at the context they may be somewhat confused, for in the passage in Isaiah, God seems to be addressing the "King of Babylon" (v. 4), and in the passage in Ezekiel, the "King of Tyre" (v. 12). Explain that back of the earthly ruler He sees the one who has used these men as his tools–his puppets; even as the Lord spoke to Satan, who was using Peter as his mouthpiece in the attempt to prevent that decisive act at Calvary which should prove the deathblow to his ambitious plans. (See Matt. 16:23.)

Explain also that many expressions in these passages that seem to indicate a human being, rather than an angel, refer to other tools–other puppets, through whom Satan manifests himself in his attempt to realize his long cherished purpose. A better understanding of these passages would eliminate many difficulties in the interpretation of prophecy.

The question may be asked, "How could this bright anointed cherub, created without iniquity and having no being to tempt him, become a sinner?" This is a mystery. It is *the* mystery. God has given us no explanation, but He simply states the fact. The approach to this condition, however, is shown us in Ezekiel 28:17: "Thine heart was lifted up because of thy beauty, thou hast corrupted thy wisdom by reason of thy brightness." The bright anointed one contemplated *his beauty, his wisdom, his brightness*—the *gifts* of God—instead of God Himself. Alas, does not this show us that self-contemplation, even the contemplation of those gifts bestowed upon us by God, is dangerous? To contemplate the gift, rather than the Giver, is the road to downfall and ruin.

THE RESULT OF SATAN'S SIN

No longer could the anointed cherub walk up and down in the midst of the stones of fire, for a sinner cannot abide in the presence of God's holiness. (See Isa. 33:14-15; Heb. 12:29.) Cast out from the presence of God, where did he go and what did he do? He was ejected from "heaven itself," never to return, but permitted to dwell within the bounds of his original dominion—the atmospheric or terrestrial heaven immediately surrounding the earth—from which point of vantage he could control affairs upon the earthly planet. Right here we need to remember that God created this angelic being with the power of choice. Satan had deliberately chosen to be the Sovereign Ruler of the universe. He had declared before all the angels that he was capable of such rulership, and he thought that he was. God's permissive will must therefore allow him to demonstrate his ability. Limited to that portion of the universe that had been entrusted to him, he must be permitted to enter upon his independent rulership.

God's omnipotence could crush him; but such crushing would be moral weakness in God.

SATAN'S FIRST FAILURE

The result of Satan's first experience in independent rulership is shown in verse 2 of the first chapter of Genesis. Let us read it as found in the Rotherham translation of the Old Testament, which more clearly follows the Hebrew than does the A.V. "Now the earth had become waste and wild and darkness was on the face of the roaring deep." Notice that the emphasis is upon the earth, or earthly sphere, which was the dominion of Satan. The Celestial region, above Satan's domination, was not included. The bright anointed cherub had demonstrated very clearly his inability to exercise independent government even in his own dominion.

Study these words "waste," "wild," "darkness," "roaring deep." Where was the earth full of beauty and light over which the "sons of God shouted for joy"? Who had marred God's glorious handiwork and brought about this chaotic condition? Alas, "an enemy hath done this."

Only He who creates is able to sustain that which is created, and all rulership is centered in God. Satan was a created being; therefore unable to sustain (literally hold together) his own principality and having chosen to be independent of God's rulership, he was unable to rule beneficently—therefore his complete failure.

Just how long a period of Satan's misrule was necessary to bring about this chaos, we do not know. Suffice it to say that in the thousands and thousands of years that lie between the creative act of God as recorded in Genesis 1:1 and His reconstructive work as recorded in the last phrase of verse 2, the geological ages are to be found. The teaching of geology agrees perfectly with the Bible if the latter is but understood. The glacial period and ice age are indicated in the account of the ruin, as stated in so few words in the verse that we have been considering.

No truly thoughtful mind could conceive of this verse as descriptive of the original earth as it came from the hand of God, and the geologist who studies the strata of the earth and its fossil remains must have a deep, unanswered question in his mind unless he knows his Bible.

We read in Isaiah 45:18 that God did not create the earth a "waste." "He formed it to be inhabited"; therefore now that it had been made empty and desolate, He patiently undertakes the work of reconstruction. This work is described in the remaining portion of the chapter.

THE RECONSTRUCTED EARTH

Notice that the word "create" is used only three times in the narrative. In verse 1, in connection with the original creation; in verse 21, when God brings into being animal life; and in verse 27, when the crowning object of creation, human life, appears. It is significant that this verb, which indicates "to bring into existence that which had no previous existence," is used at the points in the evolution theory that are regarded by evolutionists themselves as the missing links in their chain.

It is also interesting to study the order of created life biologically. First, vegetable life, which is simple unconscious life; then animal life, which is conscious, but not self-conscious; and last of all, human life, which is self-conscious.

The modern science of comparative anatomy reveals the fact that the proportion of brain to spinal cord in fish is 2 to 1, in reptiles 2½ to 1, birds 3 to 1, mammals 4 to 1, man 33 to 1, and this order from the lower to the higher, is indicated in the account of creation as recorded in the first chapter of Genesis, verses 20 to 28.

GOD A TRIUNE BEING

While much might be said concerning each sentence of this wonderful chapter, we are most concerned with those words that speak of the creation of man. In verse 26 we read, "And God said, Let us make man in our image after our likeness." How much is expressed in this short phrase. First, the plural pronoun used calls attention to the fact that God is a Triune Being. We must not think of the Trinity as mathematical; that would be tritheism—three Gods. The word "triune" signifies "three in one," a threefoldness. We might use a tree to illustrate this tri-unity:

> A tree has solid matter, leaves, bark and wood fibre, all of which are visible. In addition there are in the building of the tree force and law; it is force that does the building; it is law that governs the building. Hence in its essential composition the tree is a unity; and these three factors and nothing else, two of which are invisible, enter into the constitution of the tree. (L. T. Townsend, D.D.)

Dr. Haldeman suggests the three light rays as an illustration of the Trinity as follows:

> Light is constituted of three rays. These rays are distinct from each other. They do not form three lights but three rays and one light...no one ray without the other two is light. If one ray is light it is because the other two are conjoined with it....The three rays are never confounded, neither is the one light divided, but remains one light. Each ray has its separate function. The first originates, the second formulates, illuminates or manifests; the third consummates. The first ray is neither seen nor felt. The third ray is not seen but is felt; the second ray is both seen and felt.

The scientific mind will perceive the analogy at once, but perhaps the best illustration for the average person is the relation between the thought in the mind, the thought expressed in word, and the thought received into the mind of the hearer. E.g., a thought is in my mind which I wish my friend to share. Unless the thought is expressed in spoken, written or printed word, it will remain in my mind unperceived by my friend. I express my thought in words and immediately the thought is conveyed in words to the mind of my friend. The thought in the mind of my friend, the thought expressed in words, and the thought in my mind are one; but a threefoldness is at once discernible. The thought in my mind is the thought in its completeness; the thought expressed in word is the same thought but not the thought in its entirety, for my words cannot fully express my thought; while the thought in the mind of my friend is the invisible counterpart of the expressed thought.

The expression "God the Father" denotes God in His completeness; "God the Son" is God visualized; while "God the Holy Spirit" is the invisible counterpart of the manifested God. This three-foldness is true of God in connection with all of His acts; therefore while we read in Genesis 1:1 that God created the universe, we also read in John 1:3 that all things were created by the Eternal Son, the Logos—the Word—God visualized; and we also read of the work of the Holy Spirit in reference to creation. (See Job 26:13; 33:4; Gen. 1:2.) We must guard against using phraseology that would indicate three distinct personalities in the Trinity. In our thinking we must not permit ourselves to disassociate God the Father, God the Son, and God the Holy Spirit, and we must remember that no being ever has seen God, or ever will see Him, except as He is manifested in Christ, the Eternal Son. (See John 1:18.) With this in mind let us now consider these words of Genesis 1:26.

MAN CREATED IN THE "IMAGE" OF GOD

What is meant by "image" and "likeness"? As we study this expression we see that these two words are not synonymous; the former word refers more especially to the invisible part of man—the inner man—while the latter indicates the visible part, i.e., the outer man or body. The inner man was in some way created like God; we may reverently say, patterned after Him; yet how and to what extent we need to understand.

Let us carefully examine this subject, remembering that the failure to correctly interpret this passage is the root error of many systems of religious and philosophic thought.

God is a thinking, choosing, loving Being, and all of His activities are for the realization of a well-defined purpose which shall completely satisfy His heart; therefore in creating man in His image, we may clearly see that He created him a being capable of making a definite choice concerning a perceived goal which should completely satisfy the longing of his heart as well as the heart of God.

In other words, man was created a thinking, choosing, loving being; but we must remember that man's thinking, choosing, loving is on the plane of *created* life, while God's thinking, choosing, loving is on the plane of *Uncreated* Life far above. We must keep the two planes distinct, separate, if we would think clearly and logically.

We have said that all of God's activities are for the realization of a well-defined purpose which shall completely satisfy His heart. Let us ask then, What was His purpose in creating human beings?

GOD'S PURPOSE IN CREATING HUMAN BEINGS

Without elaboration we answer *sonship.* God wanted beings who should share His Nature and return His Love. The angels were thinking, choosing beings, but they were not created with the possibility of sonship. They could lose their original sinlessness and become sinful, but they were not created to share the Uncreated Life of God which is the essential condition for sonship. Unable to share His Nature, it follows that they would never be able to return the Uncreated Love of sons, which alone would satisfy His heart.

We read that this Uncreated Love is "shed abroad" in the hearts of God's children (see Rom. 5:5), but we do not find a word in the Bible concerning the love of angels.

We now see that something more than personality, which may be defined as "self-consciousness plus self-direction," is included in this expression concerning man's creation in the image of God.

He was created with a *capacity* for life on a higher plane. In other words, the possibility of sonship inhered in his original creation. This possibility of becoming a child of God, combined with the perception of the possibility and the power to choose the Uncreated Life of God whereby sonship would be realized, constituted man a free moral agent from the moment of his creation.

Until he should use his power of choice contrary to the perceived will of God, he would possess human righteousness and holy tendencies, but he would not be a child of God—for he would not have one spark of the Uncreated Life of God.

To sum up the foregoing, we may say that the expression concerning the creation of man in the image of God means that God bestowed upon man at his creation, intellect, sensibility, will, righteousness, conscience and the capacity for sonship.

Make very plain to the class the difference between *potential* sonship, which was man's at creation, and *actual* sonship, which could be realized only through the use of his power of choice.

MAN CREATED
AFTER THE "LIKENESS" OF GOD

We will now consider the word "likeness." Notice that the expression is *"after,"* not *in* His likeness. What is the likeness of God, after which this outer man was to be fashioned? We have already seen that the Eternal Son is the manifestation of God, i.e., God visualized. Long before God the Son—the Word—was "made flesh" (John 1:14) He appeared in human *form* again and again to human beings. Judges 13:2-22 and other passages in the Old Testament plainly reveal this fact. Now it was after this glorious form that the body was modeled. Yet here again we must keep the two planes of life distinct and separate. This glorious form was upon the plane of Uncreated Life; man's was upon the plane of created life, far below. Man could never become God in His essential Deity, but it was possible for him to choose to partake of His Life which would glorify the human clay. We read that the human body of the Last Adam (see 1 Cor. 15:45), the Lord Jesus Christ, was thus glorified, and it is after *this glorified likeness* that the first man was patterned; therefore God's objective in connection with the creation of the first Adam was the glorified Last Adam.

At this point exhibit a piece of white cardboard uniform in size with that illustrating Uncreated Life, having a short vertical line beginning some distance from the top and terminating in a small circle, while the words "Created Life" appear above, and "The First Adam," below. (See Fig. 2.)

Hang the two symbols side by side that the marked difference may strike the eye. Ask the members of the class to state these differences, and drill them in the following statements:

Uncreated Life has no beginning and no end. It is self-existent and unchangeable.

Created Life has a definite beginning. It is bestowed by God, is dependent upon God and is subject to change.

Explain that the circle upon the card containing the symbol of Created human life denotes man's endless existence. Do not allow the class to confuse endless existence with immortality. Strictly speaking, only Uncreated Life is immortal. (See 1 Tim. 6:16.)

The teacher may call attention to the three verbs that are used in the account of the creation of man. The first verb "make," verse 26, *asah* (Hebrew), signifies "to fashion or to prepare." The second is found in Genesis 2:7, "formed"—the Hebrew word *yatsar*, meaning to mold as a potter does the clay. The third is found in Genesis 1:27, "created": The Hebrew *bara* signifies to call into existence that which has had no previous existence.

We may picture the LORD God, the Eternal Son, the manifested God, forming the body of the first man out of the dust of the earth that He had previously created; then imparting to the lifeless clay the human life-principle and *creating* at the same instant the wonderful inner man so prepared that it could choose His Life and be to His glory, joy and satisfaction. Notice that the expression "the breath of life" does not indicate the impartation of Uncreated Life. It simply denotes the impartation of the human life-principle. Compare Genesis 2:7 with Genesis 6:17; 7:15, 21-22.

In Isaiah 43:7 we find these three verbs used as in this account of man's creation that we have been considering.

Picture the glory and dignity of man, and impress upon the class that no human life existed in the original earth which Lucifer had brought into a chaotic condition. Not until this last day of God's reconstructive work did human life appear. The careful use of the verb "create" argues against the existence of human life prior to Adam, and no fossil human remains have ever been found as dating back to a more remote period, although many fossil remains of animals belonging to a far earlier period than the creation of man have been found.

MAN'S TRIPARTITE BEING

The terms "inner man" and "outer man," or their equivalents, are employed in modern psychology, but the psychology of the Bible is more analytical inasmuch as it indicates a subdivision of the invisible part of man, thus teaching us that man is not dichotomous but is a trichotomous being. We find this plainly taught in 1 Thessalonians 5:23 and indicated in Hebrews 4:12 and Luke 1:46-47.

This tripartite being may be illustrated by a third piece of cardboard containing three circles. Within the inner circle print the word "spirit." Within the second circle (surrounding the first) place the word "soul," and within the outer circle the word "body." (See Fig. 3.)

Explain that the spirit is the seat of God-consciousness, the soul the seat of self-consciousness, and the body of world or sense-consciousness.

With the spirit we know God and our relation to Him and our

relation morally to every created object. With our soul powers—the intellect, sensibilities (affections, emotions) and will—we are able to deal with the intuitions of the spirit, the claims of these various soul faculties and the record of the bodily senses.

"The spirit of man," not the soul, is said to be "the candle of the Lord" (Prov. 20:27). Caution the class in reference to a careless use of these terms. Do not say "soul" when "spirit" is meant and *vice versa.* Avoid the phrase "body, soul and spirit," as it inverts the Divine order of arrangement. In a normal condition the powers of the spirit control the powers of soul and body. To illustrate, the spirit may be compared to the mistress; the soul, to the housekeeper; the body, to the servant. Invert this order and the result is a disordered household.

Many persons seem to think that spirit and soul are synonymous and feel that any attempt to teach differentiation along this line is unnecessary. Perhaps the best argument in favor of such teaching is the fact that the Bible reveals such differentiation. While it is not always easy to clearly discern the reason for the use of these words in some passages, yet a deeper study of the passages in question would doubtless reveal much that a superficial reading might overlook.

It is lamentably true that the failure to give this subject the study that it deserves has resulted in much that is "soulish" being regarded as "spiritual."

The outer man, or body, was formed for the purpose of manifesting the wonderful powers of the invisible inner man; hence the delicate relation existing between them.

While the powers of soul and spirit remained normal and poised as created, the body would manifest an unchanged existence; but should the Uncreated Life of God enter the spirit of man, it would soon permeate the soul powers, and as a result of this transformation of the inner man, the earthy particles of the body would experience a change that would eliminate the possibility of death and corruption.

On the other hand, if the powers of the inner man experienced disorder and darkness as the result of a changed attitude of dependence upon God, the inherent possibility of death in the body of dust would no longer be held in abeyance, but the entire physical part of man would undergo dissolution and corruption.

Before proceeding to the next subject, let us consider what wonderful beings came into existence when God created the first human pair. And here let us observe that while we have thus far spoken only of the creation of the man, we must remember that the personality of Eve was as truly *created* as was that of Adam.

SUPERIORITY OF THE FIRST HUMAN PAIR

We are inclined to look down from the heights of our fancied superiority upon this first pair, as pitifully ignorant of all that the ages have bestowed upon us in accumulated wisdom and knowledge. Alas, how mistaken we are. The first man with intuitive knowledge easily performed, unaided, humanly speaking, what the scientific man of today is unable to do until he has spent years of diligent study and has received help from countless human sources. Notice in verses 19 and 20 of the second chapter of Genesis that the LORD God brought the various animals that He had created to Adam "to see what *he* would call them: and whatsoever Adam called every living creature, that was the name thereof." Where is the scientific man of today who could perform this feat in classification?

If we could but look upon the first pair, fresh from the creative hand of God, with powers of spirit strong and unsullied, soul powers poised and vigorous, bodily powers unimpaired and free, we would exclaim, "Alas, how are we fallen."

NATURAL ENVIRONMENT OF ADAM AND EVE

We now need to examine the natural environment of the first created pair. We read in Genesis 2:8, "The LORD God planted a garden eastward in Eden; and there He put the man whom He had created." Can we imagine the beauty and fertility of this garden? We often gaze upon beautiful landscapes, and they please and satisfy the eye until some decaying branch, some withered leaf, some stray bramble or weed causes us to realize that after all, the beauty is marred by imperfections. We admire the wonderful beauty of the rose and delight in its fragrance, but alas, its thorn causes us pain. How different was this garden. No thorns, no thistles, brambles, briars or noxious weeds. No dead or dying trees and shrubs, but every bit of vegetation fresh, lovely, normal, perfect. Our eyes have never gazed upon the natural world free from abnormal conditions.

Our attention is particularly drawn to the trees of this garden, of which there seem to be three distinct kinds, in respect to the purpose of God in their creation; for we read in verse 9 that the LORD God made "to grow every tree that is pleasant to the sight," i.e., shade trees—indicating that God delights to gratify the perception of beauty with which He has endowed man—and trees "good for food," i.e., fruit and nut trees which furnished man all that he needed for physical sustenance; and "the tree of life also in the midst of the garden, and the tree of knowledge of good and evil." Evidently these last named trees have some other use than to furnish food for the body or emotional satisfaction to the soul of man. We may ask then, "For what purpose were they placed there?"

In answering this question notice that the tree of life is first mentioned and described as occupying the most conspicuous place in the garden—"in the *midst* of the garden." The other tree, "the tree of the knowledge of good and evil," evidently occupied a less exalted position, as if the Creator had designed that the tree of life in its prominence should render the other less conspicuous. All this is very suggestive.

We also notice that God had given free permission to eat of the tree of life but had strictly forbidden them to partake of the other tree and had told them what the penalty of disobedience would be. (See Gen. 2:16-17.) Why the permission in one case and the prohibition in the other?

THE TREE OF LIFE

Is it not probable that the same LORD God who gave to Moses the plan of that wonderful tabernacle in the wilderness, every appointment of which was a symbol of Eternal Truth, and who instituted that elaborate system of sacrificial offerings, every detail of which spoke of Him in connection with His redeeming work at Calvary, should even here at the very beginning of human history teach by symbol the truths which He wished them to know?

Can we not believe that He, who should later break bread prepared by human hands and use the same to symbolize His broken body, and who should take wine pressed from the grapes by human feet to symbolize His shed blood, should here in the Garden of Eden, before His incarnation, select the tree in the midst of the garden as a symbol of God's Uncreated Life stored in Himself for human beings? And could not our first parents with their wonderful powers of spirit and mind—powers fresh from the creative hand of God—have understood this symbol sufficiently to penetrate the same and choose the Life which was actually manifested in the glorious One who talked with them in the garden? Who can doubt it? Yet we plainly see that as yet they had not partaken of this tree. In other words, they had not made their choice in reference to Uncreated Life, or Eternal Life as it is more frequently termed; for had they eaten of the tree of life, then they would have received the Life of God which was for them in the Eternal Son, through simple faith. Thus immediately they would have become children of God, and through the continual appropriation of the provision for their transformation, eventually they would have become "conformed to the image of the Eternal Son."

ADAM NOT A SON OF GOD

Impress upon the class that the first Adam was not a son of God. Biologically we see why not. He did not possess the same kind of life. There is a mistaken idea that Redemption restores man to the unfallen plane of the First Adam. Sad indeed were this the case, for we should know nothing of sonship. Redemption places us upon the plane that Adam and Eve might have known, i.e., sonship through the Eternal Son, had they used their power of choice Godward. Notice also that if Adam and Eve had become children of God by choosing Eternal Life—the Uncreated Life of God in the Eternal Son—they could not have transmitted this Life to their children. They would have transmitted sinless human life with holy tendencies, but their children would have had to use their power of choice in reference to Uncreated Life, individually—for *Uncreated Life is always a gift from God.*

As God had created man with the capacity for Life on a higher plane, and the power to choose it, and had endowed him with moral perception of a high order, we see that the environment of man must include provision for the use of these exalted powers; hence the two trees of Paradise which we have been considering.

Much time might be spent in studying the various details of the description of this wonderful "garden of God," but we will hastily summarize in saying that the LORD God had placed the first created pair amid ideal surroundings, had empowered them to exercise dominion over the earthly creation (Gen. 1:28), and had provided everything that they needed for their powers of spirit, soul and body. Well might Milton exclaim, "O earth, how like to heaven!"

MAN'S MORAL TEST

We now come to a narrative that would be utterly unintelligible had not God given us the clue to a clear understanding of the same through other portions of His Written Word. Let the entire class read Genesis 3:1-7. What is the meaning of this strange temptation scene? Who is the tempter? Apparently it is the bright-hued serpent twining around the only object in the garden concerning which God had imposed prohibitive commands. However, as we read the words uttered by the serpent, we realize that this reptile cannot be the real tempter; for reptiles are on the plane of animal life, which we have found to be below the plane of self-consciousness; and not only do these few words reveal self-consciousness but marvelous intellectual powers, a dominant will and God-consciousness as well. We must look elsewhere, then, for the real but invisible tempter who is using the serpent as his mouthpiece, his tool. Eliminating the entire animal creation, we ask, "Who can the tempter be?" Is there any other human being present, who, for some subtle reason, is striving to lead Adam and Eve to disobey God's commands? Most certainly not; for this man and woman are the only human beings in God's great universe. Would God tempt them to do that which He had expressly commanded them not to do, and the fatal results of which He well knew? Unthinkable. God tempts no one. Who can the tempter be?

Is there any other plane of life which might furnish the tempter? Only the angelic plane; therefore we conclude that the invisible tempter is an angel and evidently an angelic being of high rank. Have we any clue as to his identity? The careful student of psychology would suggest at once that the language of the tempter bears a strong resemblance to that uttered ages before by Lucifer. The same attitude of assumed equality with God is indicated; the same wilful disregard of His Sovereign commands.

The thinking person would also perceive that Lucifer, or Satan, as we will now call him, had a definite purpose in connection with the human beings whom God had created. He knew that God had given man dominion over the earthly creation, and he could readily see that if man remained in dependence upon his Creator, he would be able to exercise earthly dominion in such a manner that no part of the earthly sphere could be controlled by his fallen powers. Satan also reasoned that if human beings exercised dominion in the earthly sphere, the result might be that they would become empowered to eject him from his place in the atmospheric heaven, and thus his ambitious plans would come to naught; and the awful judgment which God pronounced upon him ages before would become a terrible reality.

His first failure in independent government—the transformation of God's beautiful earth into chaos—evidently had wrought no change in his character nor had it destroyed his ambition. Doubtless he felt disappointment and chagrin over his failure but no repentance; and after God's reconstructed earth appeared, he was as ready as ever to become its ruler. In view of these facts and conditions, we are forced to believe that Satan is the invisible tempter who is using the Serpent as his mouthpiece.

This temptation scene will bear much study. Let us carefully note the setting that we may the better understand the results. The scene is the wonderful garden of God with its waving trees, fragrant flowers, sparkling water and every object of natural beauty. Satan is a wonderful strategist. He has planned deliberately and well concerning every detail of this decisive moment in the history of the human race. First, he has selected an opportune moment when Eve is alone. (We cannot help wondering if he had not previously attracted the attention of Adam to some other spot.) Then he has selected the most peculiarly striking member of the animal creation to attract the attention of Eve and to serve as his spokesman. The bright-hued serpent, which in primeval days was erect and doubtless able to glide gracefully from tree to tree, was used to draw Eve's attention to the forbidden object.

As we examine the account before us in this chapter, we do not see the tree of life as the center of the story, nor do we find it mentioned. Evidently the attention of Eve is directed by her questioner to the other tree, and so absorbed does she become in contemplating it, that in speaking of the tree "in the midst of the garden," the fruit of which she had been forbidden to eat, she seems to have forgotten the tree in the midst of the garden of which she was permitted to freely eat. (Compare Gen. 3:2-3 with 2:16-17.)

We can imagine her standing with her back to the tree of life at this moment, gazing at the bright, sinuous body of the serpent twined around the forbidden tree, which, doubtless, she had not permitted herself to look upon except with awe, up to this moment, but which now fascinated her with its wondrous beauty. Evidently the thought of disobedience had not entered into her mind until it was projected by the tempter, as a psychological analysis of verse 3 reveals.

Her addition to God's prohibition, expressed in the words "neither shall ye touch it," reveals the state of her mind. Her purpose to obey was so strong that she would not *even touch* the forbidden object; doubtless she would not fix her gaze upon it. This is the normal attitude of an innocent mind. We see it today in very conscientious children and adults; and if this is true of persons who have inherited a sinful nature, how much stronger must this attitude have been in one who possessed a sinless nature. The expression, "lest ye die," does not indicate an attempt to tone down the result of disobedience. "Lest" does not mean peradventure. She simply stated what the result of disobedience would be.

But now for the first time, the thought of disobedience to God's command is presented to her mind and finds lodgment there. And yet so subtle is the working of the tempter, that eating of the forbidden fruit does not seem to be direct disobedience. Satan has so staged the scene that he has caused her to forget the "tree of life." He has gained control of her eyes; he has projected his thought of disobedience into her mind; he has caused her to question God's Word, and now he completely dazzles her mind so that she accepts his word instead of God's and uses her will exactly as he had planned.

Later he uses Eve in tempting Adam to make his choice—and Satan's object is gained. He has succeeded in tempting Adam and Eve to use their power of choice in such a way that the original possibility of sonship is removed, their sinless condition is changed to that of sinfulness, and they have become his servants, his slaves.

In portraying this garden scene and its awful results we should carefully avoid any expression that would lessen the solemnity of this direful moment in the history of the human race. The allusion to *Eve eating the apple* betrays a sad lack of appreciation of the tremendous consequences attending the act of the Mother of our race, and it also shows lack of logical thought in connection with the vital truths of God's Word.

The teacher should now call attention to the penalty attached to the prohibition. God had said, "in the day thou eatest thereof thou shall surely die." What did He mean by this? Surely not immediate dissolution of the body, for Adam and Eve lived many, many years after their fall.

WHAT GOD MEANS BY DEATH

The scientific definition of death helps us to perceive His meaning. It is as follows: "Death is the falling out of correspondence with environment." The following illustration will help the class to better understand this subject. Here is an eye of a human being, seemingly perfect in structure, wide open, apparently able to see any object placed before it. The objects of nature, bathed in bright sunlight surround it, but there is no response from the eye. It does not see; for the optic nerve is severed. It is *dead* to the beauty before it.

Here is a person whose ears are completely deafened. Birds are singing, bells are ringing, voices speaking, but those ears do not respond to the sound waves that are carrying melody to other ears which are open to receive the same. They are *dead* to the sounds.

Upon the very day of Adam and Eve's disobedience, sin severed the delicate intuitive knowledge of God in the spirit of Adam and Eve. They failed to respond to Him who was their Environing Presence. They were *dead* to God. Therefore, we see that a human being may be moral, educated, refined, strong and vigorous in mind and body, yet dead to God. He may even know many things about God and talk about Him, preach about Him, write books about Him and still be dead to Him—without response to the voice of His

Spirit. This helps us to understand the meaning of such passages as 1 Timothy 5:6; Ephesians 5:14; Romans 8:6.

This classification of human beings into the groups, the "dead" and the "alive," will appeal to the scientific man, for in like manner he classifies all objects. Were a large number of objects placed before him he would not put the objects of beauty in one pile and those devoid of beauty in another, as a child would do; but he would examine each in reference to the possession of life. Consequently one collection of objects he would label "alive," the other "dead."

God does not classify upon the basis of moral beauty or "good works." Concerning each human being He asks, "Has he *Life? Is he alive unto Me?*"

The death process established in the spirit of our first parents was quickly manifested throughout the whole of the inner man, and after a time the possibility of dissolution of the body, which had been held in abeyance while man remained obedient and dependent before the Fall, became an actuality. The bodies so wonderfully formed of the dust of the earth and which might have been glorified, now returned to dust. The teacher should now place a black disc containing the three circles symbolizing spirit, soul and body, over the white circles symbolizing this tripartite being of man. (See Fig. 4.)

THE LAW OF HEREDITY

We now need to notice a phrase used several times in the account of the creative work of God as found in the first chapter of Genesis. We first find it in verse 21: "And God created great whales (literally sea monsters) and every living creature that moveth, which the waters brought forth abundantly, *after their kind,* and every winged fowl *after its kind*"; and again in verse 24 we read, "And God said, Let the earth bring forth the living creature *after its kind,* cattle, and creeping thing, and beast of the earth *after its kind.*

And God made the beast of the earth *after its kind,* and cattle *after their kind,* and every thing that creepeth upon the earth *after its kind.*"

Science tells us that in the original germ of all animal life no difference is discernible. One bit of protoplasm develops into the beast, another into the bird, still another into the reptile. More wonderful still, the original germ of vegetable, animal and human life is precisely the same viewed through the microscope, or analyzed by the chemist. But the scientific man cannot tell us why one germ produces an oak, another a lion, still another a man. Evidently there is a distinct life-principle in each germ, and these various life-principles follow an unvarying law in the reproduction of the form of life which it is to manifest. What a relief to turn from the limited knowledge of the scientific world to these simply stated words of God. His creative power brought into being these various forms of life, and their reproduction is but *an extension of His creative act.* (See this statement set forth in the wonderful poetry of Psalm 104:30.) Many have been the attempts to prove the theory of "spontaneous generation," but these attempts have resulted in complete failure. Theory after theory has been advanced and experiment upon experiment has been made to solve the great problems connected with the origin of life upon this planet and the mysteries of its reproduction. Evolutionists have felt at times that their elaborate researches were to be rewarded with success; but no keenly logical mind among them now desires to say that their chain is complete, for there are fatally weak links which perplex and discourage.

Bearing in mind the thought already advanced, that reproduction of life is the extension of God's creative act, it is not difficult to perceive that a law has been established by God Himself from which there can be no deviation. Each form of life will be reproduced "after its kind," so long as the reproduction of that life continues.

Another self-evident fact we will note. Each form of life has a definite goal which the invisible but inherent life-principle causes it to reach. In scientific phraseology this goal is the *type* to which it is to be conformed. Type, as used in this connection, may be defined as "the aggregate of characteristic qualities." We see from what we have considered, how impossible it is for life on one plane to generate life on another plane. All that any life-principle can do is to bring to manifestation and maturity the life on that particular plane; e.g., the life-principle in the lily bulb will produce the lily life, and, if unhindered, will cause all the characteristics of that life to reach their perfection; but the life-principle in the lily can never produce bird life, nor can the life-principle in the egg of the bird do more than to cause the manifestation of the bird life. The bird life may reach its goal but it can go no higher. In other words, the bird may spread its wings and fly far up in the air; it may sing its sweetest song; but it can never generate human life. Human life, in turn, can only reproduce itself. It cannot generate life on a higher plane—the Uncreated Life of God.

We will now apply this law of heredity to Adam and Eve in their fallen condition. What are the characteristics of the life that they must reproduce? First, it is created (not self-existent) life; second, it is human life, not the Life of God; third, it is sinful, not sinless, life; therefore we may say that the children of Adam and Eve will come into the world with sinful, created, human life. The poison of sin is in the human germ, and it will be manifested with each unfolding life. It cannot be otherwise. It follows, then, that every descendant of Adam and Eve will enter the world with the same kind of life—i.e., sinful, created, human life. The words of the Apostle Paul in Romans 5:12 are fully in accord with this inflexible law of heredity: "Through one man sin entered into the world, and death by sin; and so death passed upon all men for that all sinned."

We must remember that we have found sin to be far more than an act, and we have seen the relation between sin and death; therefore the law of heredity and the "law of sin and death" run parallel throughout the world of human beings.

Before proceeding to another subject the teacher will do well to review what has already been presented in reference to sin. Have the pupils copy or commit to memory the following summary:

Sin is an attitude of wilful, deliberate resistance to the authority of God. The manifestations of this attitude are *sins*.

Sin originated with Satan ages before man was created. The immediate results of Satan's sin were,
(a) Banishment forever from the Presence of God.
(b) Loss of dominion.
(c) Bondage to fear.

In reference to the last clause, explain that the awful words of judgment uttered by God to the first sinner cannot be forgotten by him. Satan remembers them well and he fears exceedingly; yet he is ever seeking to prevent the complete execution of the sentence of doom.

The result of Satan's sin in connection with the earthly sphere over which he had been given dominion, was a disordered, chaotic earth.
Satan tempted Adam and Eve to sin.
The immediate results of their sin were,
(a) Death, i.e., separation from God—unresponsiveness to Him.
(b) Loss of dominion.
(c) Bondage to Satan.

The result of man's sin in connection with the earthly creation over which God had given him dominion, is a disordered, suffering, dying condition in the human, animal and vegetable planes of life. (See Rom. 8:22.)

It will not be necessary at this time to enlarge upon the results of sin in connection with atmospheric and topographical changes, but we are justified in saying that sin has so changed and disfigured the earthly creation that we see its traces wherever we look. Not only in every human being, but in every member of the animal creation and in every bit of vegetation—we are forced to realize the results of man's sin. The wonder is that with "earth's king gone astray," the earth has not again become "waste and wild." But God has sustained because He had a purpose concerning the human race and a plan to be worked out in this sin-cursed world.

Let us now consider this great Eternal Purpose for the human race more in detail. Ask the class to read Romans 8:29-30 and Ephesians 1:3-5.

PECULIAR BLENDING OF FIGURES

As we carefully ponder these words we find that two figures are employed: the architectural and the parental, and they are peculiarly blended. The word "predestinate" means "to mark out." Just as an architect conceives in his mind a wonderful group of buildings, and proceeds to draw a plan of the same—a plan showing each detail in its relation to the whole and to the various portions—so God, the Great Architect, has outlined in His Written Word, His wondrous, glorious conception of a "city" composed of many buildings, each one of which is a glorified human being—"the city which hath foundation, whose Architect and Builder is God" (Heb. 11:10), and which is for His (not man's) dwelling place. This city is beautifully described in the Revelation, and while we must remember that the Holy Spirit is employing a figure of speech in all of these passages, yet we must discern the blessed truth that the figure is seeking to reveal.

Now let us look at the other figure, the parental, and the peculiar blending of this with the architectural figure that we have just considered. In Ephesians 1:5 we see that the individual buildings in this city are called "sons" and we are shown that the ultimate purpose of God is this—that the human beings whom He has created shall partake of His Life which He has stored for them in the Eternal Son, and that this Life shall so transform them that eventually they will be conformed to His Image. Hebrews 2:10 points to this consummation.

We see then, that God's Eternal Purpose for human beings is Sonship through the Eternal Son, and that these glorified individuals collectively will form a community which is spoken of as a "city" (see Rev. 21:2-3, 22-23) for His indwelling; or will constitute a "vast circle of brothers" in the Father's Home.

THE GREATEST PROBLEM IN THE UNIVERSE

We now stand face to face with the greatest problem in the universe: How can human beings dead to God and "dead in trespasses and sins" become children of God and eventually "sons brought to glory"? Biologically, it is an impossibility; for we know that life on each plane can only reproduce itself; it cannot generate life on a higher plane. Man cannot attain to the Life of God by any self-effort. Science agrees perfectly with the Bible in declaring, "that which is born of the flesh is flesh; and that which is born of the Spirit is spirit" (John 3:6). Life on the various planes must forever remain distinct, apart; therefore, so far as any effort of man is concerned, the entire human race must forever remain upon the plane of sinful life. "All have sinned," therefore all have "come short of the glory of God" (Rom. 3:23).

God is an absolutely holy Being. He cannot tolerate sin. He cannot excuse it. We could not worship a God who would treat sin lightly. Impress upon the class the *awfulness* of sin but in such a manner as to enable them to perceive that there is a *law* of sin which, like any natural law is followed by inevitable results. (See Rom. 8:2, last phrase.) Do not permit them to indulge in the weak, illogical reasoning of many persons who say that "God is too loving to punish sinners." Is it lack of love in God that permits a person to fall when he has thrown himself over the edge of a precipice? No, the force of gravity is irresistible. Is it unloving in God when the hand that has deliberately been held in the flame is burned? No, we are familiar with the working of natural laws and we recognize their inflexibility.

Lead the class to see that God's punishment of sin is not

arbitrary—rather that it is the inevitable result of an inflexible law, an illustration of cause and effect. Much harm has been done in representing God as angrily punishing the sinner in an arbitrary manner, instead of presenting Him as the Holy, loving God grieving over sinful human beings who are experiencing the fatal results of the working of the absolute, inflexible "law of sin and death" in their lives. The everlasting separation of sinners from God must be the logical result of sin.

God's holiness and man's sinfulness can never coalesce. God can never be anything else than holy; man can never be anything else than sinful, in his natural condition.

We see, then, that the claims of God's holiness would necessitate the removal of sinners from His immediate presence and would render impossible any fellowship or relationship between them.

But not only is God a holy Being; He is a loving Being also. "God is Love" (1 John 4:8). The claims of His Love as well as the claims of His Holiness must be considered. God's Love yearns over the race of sinners. He loves them with His own Uncreated Love which can never change. He longs to clasp them in His arms and call them sons.

Here are distinctly opposing claims. God's holiness must say to sinners "depart from Me"; God's Love must open His arms to receive them. How are these opposing claims to be reconciled? Only in a judicial manner, i.e., in the form of legal justice. To illustrate: Two men have opposing claims, therefore they resort to the court of justice. Each tells his story while the judge patiently listens; then he renders his *judgment* which is the official declaration concerning the truth of the statements submitted to him for consideration, based upon the laws of the state.

Let us bear in mind that the word judgment in the Scriptures is used in this vindicatory sense, rather than in the vindictive. It is a "setting right." With this explanation in mind, let us consider what the judgment in connection with the opposing claims of God's holiness and His love will be. It may be stated as follows: The claims of God's love are just, and His love has the right to effect any possible change in the status of sinful human beings that will cause them to satisfy His heart; but this change of status must also uphold and satisfy His holiness.

Let us now consider what this change of status would involve. First, it would necessitate a new life-principle, nature, heredity; second, the operation of a higher law than the "law of sin and death" must be realized; third, deliverance from the sphere and control of Satan must be effected.

We also perceive that this change of status must be accomplished in such a manner that God's holiness would be magnified and His moral rule vindicated throughout the universe.

But not only must the sin question of the human race be settled judicially, it must be settled decisively, i.e., in one decisive act. And it must be settled *effectually*. In other words, the "setting right" must not omit a single detail of this great problem.

We are now ready to ask, What must be the nature of the single decisive act whereby such changes as those we have been considering may be effectually accomplished? The answer may be concisely stated in the following sentence: It must be a *manifestation of suffering upon the part of God, commensurate with the result of man's sin.* As we carefully examine this sentence we see that in no other way can the unchanging Love and Holiness of God be reconciled; and in no other way can each be fittingly expressed. This manifestation of suffering Love and absolute Holiness is also the only way whereby sinful man may become a child of God.

Perhaps the following illustration may help the class to more fully perceive this point. A man has a friend whom he truly loves. He meets him frequently and enjoys his society. He looks forward to many years of friendly intercourse; but one day he is shocked to find that his friend is guilty of embezzlement upon a large scale

and has lost all in wild speculation. His fine sense of honesty re-
coils from further intimacy with the man, but his love suffers
keenly over such a break in friendship. He pities the man while he
despises his sin. How can these opposite emotions be reconciled?
Only by an act which will give expression to each. Consequently
he calls upon his friend, finds out the extent of his wrongdoing,
disposes of his own property and with the proceeds makes good
the losses of the innocent victims of his friend's dishonesty. We see
that the love of the man and his sense of honesty have found expression in this sacrificial act; and, if in addition to this, the heart
of his friend is touched and he is truly repentant, then this
self-imposed act of the man is a faint picture of the Redeeming
grace extended to the sinner.

We now need to consider this expression of God's Love and
Holiness more in detail. It is obvious that it must be in such form
as would enable sinful man to perceive its meaning. Therefore God
must clothe Himself with humanity, that humanity might understand God's heart. We can readily see, however, that not all of God
could be covered with humanity's form. God is Infinite and the
created universe could not confine Him. But the Eternal Son—the
manifested God—laid aside His independent Divine Power and
much of His glory, but NOT His Divine *nature*, and clothed Himself
with humanity as with a garment.

A UNIQUE PERSONALITY – THE GOD-MAN

We find this fact plainly stated in John 1:14, also in Philippians
2:5-7. This uniting of two planes of life in one personality would
present to the world a unique Being—"The God-Man."

At this point the teacher should call attention to the first word
in the Bible in reference to this unique personality. Have the class
read Genesis 3:14-15. Explain that the LORD God is pronouncing a
curse upon the literal serpent in verse 14. This reptile had been the
tool of Satan and was to experience changed conditions; its degra-
dation doubtless being intended by God to serve as an object

lesson to the end of time. Other animals are to return to their original condition in the glorious Millennial Age, but the serpent will continue to glide on its sinuous way in the dust, although its venom will have been removed. (See Isa. 65:25; 11:6-8.)

In verse 15 the LORD God is speaking to the being who had used the serpent as his mouthpiece. This being we have already found to be Satan who had tempted Adam and Eve to sin. Notice very carefully the words that are uttered, for this verse contains the germ of all Redemptive revelation: "Enmity will I put between thee and the woman, and between thy seed and her seed; He shall crush thy head but thou shall crush his heel" (Rotherham translation). As we read and re-read, we perceive that the personal pronoun "He" is the emphatic word. Evidently a unique, strong personality is indicated. This personality is said to be the "seed of the woman," an unusual expression considered biologically; for when natural generation is mentioned, the expression "seed of man" is used. The fact that no human father is indicated and that this *seed* is to "crush" the head of Satan, would argue that He was to be a super-man. We see also that the crushing of the head of Satan would be to his ambitious power and rule what the crushing of the head of a little serpent would be—a death blow. And we see also that the crushing of the heel of the strong one, in the act of crushing the head of the serpent, would mean that all of the venomous power of the serpent would be directed against the heel, causing untold suffering.

Let us now see if we can find other passages corroborating this peculiar expression, "the seed of the woman." In Isaiah 7:14 we read these words: "Behold a (*the* in the original) virgin shall conceive, and bear a son, and shall call his name Immanuel." This name is very suggestive. It implies the uniting of two planes of life: the Uncreated Life of God and the created life of humanity. The word *Immanuel* means "God with us." The *us* refers to humanity, and the force of the expression is *God in humanity*.

In Isaiah 9:6 we find "us" again used. "Unto us (i.e., humanity) a child is born"; but notice carefully the next phrase—"A son is *given*," not born; implying that His origin is above the plane of humanity. And notice the name given Him: "The Wonderful Counselor, The Mighty God, The Everlasting Father, The Prince of Peace." Could any child of human origin bear such a name?

In Micah 5:2 we find where this God-Man is to be born. In reading this passage call attention to the last phrase: "Whose goings forth have been from of old, from everlasting," and compare with the last phrase of Psalm 90:2.

Now let us turn to Matthew 1:18-25 where we find the birth of Immanuel, in Bethlehem, recorded. Also read the beautiful account of His birth as recorded by Luke, the physician. (See Luke 2:1-20.) No wonder that the angels shouted for joy, for God had clothed Himself with humanity, that He might redeem a sinful human race.

A fourth cardboard symbol should now be shown. This is of uniform size with those already used and contains a large gilt star placed over three circles like those on card 3. A metal fastener is attached to the star and is inserted in the card. Above the star should be placed the words *The God-Man*. Underneath the star in smaller letters may be printed, "The Last Adam." (See Fig. 5.) Explain the latter expression by calling attention to 1 Corinthians 15:45, 47; also link this expression with His human name Jesus, meaning *Savior*. (See Matt. 1:21.) Point to the white circles as symbolizing His humanity, and make clear to the class that He really partook of our human nature. Have Hebrews 2:14-18 read, also Hebrews 4:14-15. Dwell upon the fact that He needed food for the sustenance of His human body and sleep for its refreshment. Call attention to various passages in the Gospels that prove these facts. Point to the star as symbolizing His Deity. Draw out from the class the proofs of His Deity as found in the Gospels. Let those passages be read which mention His forgiving sins and receiving worship; but be careful not to include those acts of His which were performed as *man*, exercising faith in God and in utter dependence upon Him; such as fasting in the wilderness, walking upon the water, and passing through the angry mob in Nazareth. These, and other of His recorded acts, also prove the exercise of that dominion originally given to man which the first Adam forfeited through sin, but which the Last Adam completely manifested. Also have those passages read which emphasize His dependence upon God, His Father; e.g., John 6:38; 7:16, 28-29; 8:28-29, 38, 49-50; 5:30.

It will be very helpful if the contrast between the temptation scene in the Garden of Eden and that in the wilderness is shown. A whole lesson might well be devoted to this. Notice that the Last Adam has the same tempter that overcame the First Adam. The same masterful mind that carefully planned the temptation in the beautiful garden has prepared his snare to entrap and overcome the Last Adam in the wilderness; but notice that where our first parents questioned and disobeyed God's Word, the Last Adam reiterated, "It is written," and remained firm in obedience and humble in dependence. The First Adam lost his God-given dominion when he sinned, and became the slave of Satan. The Last Adam exercised dominion and went up from the wilderness a *king*.

Right here explain to the class the meaning of dominion as used in this connection, for the subject is little understood. True dominion has for its object the highest welfare of those dominated, and has power to effect the realization of the same, choosing to do this at any cost to self. Dominion is the exact opposite of domineering, which has for its object the realization of selfish ambition at the expense of those controlled.

> God created man to be the ruler of the earth; he was to be the representative of God and a king here below. All things were to be subject to him. The idea of kingship is that it is not an authority entrusted to man by man. It does not come from below. It is a power and sovereignty given by the supreme Lord of heaven and earth. (Adolph Saphir)

Call attention to the fact that Satan forfeited his *dominion* when he sinned, and that he entered upon his *domineering* career, not as a king over his subjects, but rather as a master over his slaves.

Even an archangel is but a vassal, not an independent king, and if he does not rule aright the kingdom which has been entrusted to him, it will be given to another. (Pastor Stockmayer)

It will now readily be seen that the humanity of the God-Man is sinless, dependent and victorious; therefore He is ready to execute that Plan for the Redemption of the human race which was in the mind of God even before He created the universe. In proof of this statement we have but to remember the omniscience of God. With God it is always present tense. He has no past, no future. He saw the result of man's sin before He created him and assumed the responsibility incurred in creating a being with the power of choice. He discharged that responsibility by providing a way whereby man might use his power of choice in such a manner that he could be freed from sin and become His glorified son. Thus God's Plan of Redemption antedates the sin of man that made it necessary.

WHAT THE REDEEMER MUST DO

Let us now carefully note what the Redeemer must do in executing this Plan. First: He must become identified with the human race in its sinfulness. This means a deeper humbling. We see this indicated in Philippians 2:8. In the previous verse we read, "He emptied Himself" to be "made in the likeness of man"; but now we read, "being found in fashion as a man He *humbled* Himself, and became obedient unto death, even the death of the Cross."

Second: Identified with sinners, He must vicariously and representatively come under the operation of the law of sin and death in a substitutionary manner, that He might experience the full penalty for sin—i.e., death, or separation from God.

Third: Having representatively and substitutionally experienced the penalty, He must representatively manifest the working of a higher law, even *the law of the Spirit of Life*—the Life of God.

Fourth: As the glorified God-Man, He must become the Head of a new order of redeemed human beings, who should share His Life and eventually become conformed to His Image and be found in His Likeness.

All this, the God-Man—Jesus Christ—was ready to do; for He had said, "Lo, I come to do thy will, O God."

Part 2

GOD'S PLAN
OF REDEMPTION
FULLY ACCOMPLISHED

In entering upon the second section of these studies it is necessary that the members of the class should have a fair understanding of the subjects presented in Section One. Otherwise the execution of God's wonderful plan for the redemption of the human race will fail to be appreciated in its completeness.

THE SUFFERING TRINITY

The teacher should emphasize the fact that this Plan of Redemption is the manifestation of the suffering holy love of the Triune God and that this suffering antedated the historical manifestation at Calvary. Says Dr. Mabie in *The Divine Reason of the Cross,*

> In a deep sense God "tasted death" upon the Cross—there was a Cross in heaven ere it was set up on Calvary; a sword pierced the heart of the Heavenly Father, long before it entered the heart of Mary, Jesus' earthly mother. This premundane anguish in God was the very fount and source of the entire sacrificial life of Christ, as well as a part of it. "God so loved the world that He gave His Only Begotten Son."

This view of the suffering Trinity renders impossible the acceptance of the erroneous teaching that God in His holiness is kept from destroying the sinner only through the atoning work of the Son. Dr. Mabie continues,

> Has it been anything short of a calamity to the evangelical system that God the Father has often been shown as a distinct impassable abstract majesty, and that the Son has been set over against Him to protect the sinner from Him? Has not this conception destroyed the real Fatherhood altogether and made God to appear as chiefly concerned to preserve His abstract passionless honor, with Christ enduring all the pain of upholding this standard while man gets the benefit of it?

Let the following passages now be read to prove the foregoing statements: 2 Corinthians 5:19; 1 Timothy 3:16; Acts 20:28, last phrase. Notice the expression "which He (God) hath purchased with His own blood"—a statement proving the Deity of Jesus Christ as well as the unity of the Triune God. We are now able to better understand those passages that speak of "the Lamb foreordained before the foundation of the world" (1 Pet. 1:18-20; Rev. 13:8). Truly, "the atonement in principle and in God is dateless, but as taking effect on man it is historical though dateless" (Dr. Mabie).

THE LAMB OF GOD FORESHADOWED

We shall now examine this historical event in detail. It is interesting to note that the Old Testament Scriptures foreshadow and foretell not only the fact of a Redeeming Achievement but also the very manner in which this is to be accomplished. The sacrificial element runs through its pages like a scarlet thread. It is first seen in Genesis 3:21. Have the class read this verse thoughtfully. What were these "skins" with which the LORD God clothed the sinful pair? Call attention to Genesis 4:2, 4 as furnishing a clue. Is it not reasonable to believe that the LORD God instructed Adam to kill a lamb to provide the necessary covering? Is it not a logical inference, considering the fact that throughout the entire Bible we see the *lamb* associated with the sacrificial offering for sin? We have every reason to believe that the LORD God instructed Adam to take a lamb—perhaps a choice lamb—the one upon which he had lavished the most tender care; his in a peculiar sense—and with his own hands plunge the sharp flint into the body of the innocent, trusting animal that had done nothing worthy of death. Can we imagine the emotions of the man as the life blood flowed forth? Then, as he proceeds to fashion from its skin the covering necessitated by his sin, does he need to be told the meaning of this sacrificial death? May we not believe that he knew in the depths of his being that the life which had been sacrificed for his sin was a type—a figure of a more precious life that should be sacrificed not only to cover the results of his sin, but which should effectually deal with it?

Is it not altogether probable that the promised "seed of the woman" was now associated with the slain lamb in the mind of Adam? Did he not now understand the "crushing of the heel" to mean sacrifice upon the part of the Promised One, and the crushing of the "head" of the serpent a victorious consummation which the "seed of the woman" should realize? And as he clothed himself with the covering of the slain lamb, did he not thereby perceive that he might become identified with the Promised One, in His sacrificial work and His complete victory over sin and Satan? We do not know how much of God's Plan of Redemption was perceived by Adam and Eve, but we do know that through the illumination of God the Holy Spirit, they understood enough to put faith in God's Slain Lamb.

From this time the thought of sacrifice for sin finds lodgment in the human mind: thus we see Abel bringing his lamb for a sacrificial offering as instructed by God; and later we read of the Passover Lamb in connection with the exodus of the Israelites from Egypt, and we note the commemoration and continuance of this Paschal Offering in the tabernacle in the Wilderness and still later in the temple at Jerusalem. Indeed, throughout the Bible from Genesis to the Revelation, we find the *Slain Lamb* in symbol or in substance.

MAN'S CREATED RIGHT
TO THE TREE OF LIFE FORFEITED

We now need to read Genesis 3:22-24, a passage, which if rightly understood, conveys the precious hope of Redemption and glorious sonship to the members of the human race. Let us read the passage from the Rotherham translation: "Then said Yahweh God—Lo! man hath become like one of us, in respect of knowing good and evil. Now therefore lest he thrust forth his hand and take even of the tree of life, and eat and live to times age abiding—So Yahweh God put him forth from the Garden of Eden, to till the ground wherefrom he had been taken. So He expelled the man—and caused to dwell in front of the Garden of Eden—cherubim—and a brandishing sword flame, to keep (or guard) the way to the tree of life."

Yahweh God (or Jehovah Elohim) is translated LORD God in the A.V. This expression is not found in the Bible until after the creation of man. (See Gen. 2:4, 7.) It signifies the "Self-Existent One who reveals Himself"; or the Manifested God; therefore indicates the Eternal Son. *Yahweh,* translated Jehovah, in the Old Testament, is the Redemption name of God. It indicates Christ of the New Testament. *Elohim* is a plural noun indicating God in His complete threefoldness, as shown in Genesis 1:26, "Let *us* make," etc.; "Yahweh Elohim," as used in this passage and at least one other (Gen. 11:7), indicates this same plural form, as shown by the personal pronoun *us.*

The expression "in respect of knowing good and evil," indicates the fact of man's choosing *experimental knowledge* as the result of *independent activity,* rather than to remain in absolute dependence upon God. It was another way of declaring that the members of the human race had "turned every one to his *own* way." Verse 22 is an unfinished sentence, difficult to explain; yet if we carefully weigh all that we have previously considered in reference to the tree of life in its symbolic character, this difficult phrase becomes more intelligible. Possibly the following paraphrase will convey what was in

God's mind when He uttered these words: "Because man has chosen to eat of the tree of the knowledge of good and evil, instead of the tree of life—the eating of which would bestow Eternal Life and immortality—therefore must he be sent forth from Eden to realize the result of his choice." Attention has previously been called to the fact that "lest" does not mean peradventure. God would not send man out of Eden to deprive him of that which the tree symbolized, but that He might avert the possibility of his presuming upon his *created right* to the tree of Life—a right which he had forfeited.

THE WAY TO THE TREE OF LIFE PRESERVED

But now note the precious fact that although man has forfeited his *created* right to eat of the tree of Life, the *way* to that tree is to be kept open for him; so that if he chooses the way, he will have the *right* to the tree and be permitted to freely eat of its fruit. Carefully notice the wonderful provision made to guard this way to the tree of life. The Cherubim surrounding the tree and the revolving sword flame presented an awe-inspiring picture of God's holiness and Love in providing a way whereby sinful man should partake of His Life. But perhaps one may ask, "Why the need of such constant keeping?" Because Satan would close the way if possible. He quickly perceived that if this way were kept open for sinful man, his hold over man would be gone forever. His purposes would fail of fulfillment. What was this *way? The Sacrificial offering of God's Lamb*—God's Plan of Redemption.

SATAN SEEKS TO CLOSE THE WAY TO THE TREE OF LIFE

From the moment that Satan perceived the purpose of God, as symbolized by the guarded way to the tree which has been described, all of his corrupted wisdom and selfish power were concentrated upon one object: *to frustrate the Redemptive Plan of God.* We see his success in the case of Cain, the first child born into the world. He projects into his mind, already tainted by his sinful inheritance, the thought of substituting some other sacrificial offering than the slain lamb. Have the class read the account of the two offerings in Genesis 4:1-8 and explain the significance of each. The Rotherham translation of verses 6 and 7 is very helpful. "So then Yahweh said unto Cain, Wherefore hath it angered thee, and wherefore hath thy countenance fallen? Shall it not if thou do right be lifted up? But if thou do not right at the entrance a sin-bearer is lying." This last phrase points to the fact that the LORD God calls attention to the fact that Abel would supply him with a lamb from his flock as an offering; indeed the Hebrew text seems to indicate that he was longing to do so, for he penetrated the symbol,* and in offering his sacrifice, he manifested faith in God's Lamb. (See Heb. 11:4.) Cain was given every opportunity to follow Abel's example, but he deliberately refused, and in him we see the first sinner to refuse God's Plan of Redemption and put faith in God's Slain Lamb.

We next observe Satan's attempt to prevent the execution of the Redemptive Plan, in the fact that he leads Cain to murder his brother, thus planning to make void the promise of the seed of the woman; for Satan could not look into the future and see the birth of this promised Seed in Bethlehem. Doubtless he, as well as Adam and Eve, expected this Coming One to be a child of Eve.

The major portion of the Old Testament deals with the history of the race, tribe and family from which the Redeemer should come, and it is interesting to notice the efforts of Satan in each generation to render futile the prophecies concerning the birth of this Promised One. There were times when the royal line of David seemed extinct, but God overruled as in the case of Joash. (See 2 Chron. 22:10-12.) Idolatry and wickedness of every kind brought

---

* Note: Of course the teacher will explain more fully, if necessary, the relation between the symbol and the Reality, as some persons cannot readily interpret symbolic teaching.

disaster to the nation, yet God's word concerning the promised Redeemer was literally fulfilled. After the birth of the God-Man, Satan sought to slay Him. After His baptism, he sought to master Him through subtle temptation. All through the earthly ministry of the God-Man, Satan sought to hinder, to render inoperative, to prevent the work given Him to do. In the garden of Gethsemane, Satan sought to take away that life which the God-Man had said He was to "lay down of Himself" for His sheep. (See John 10:14-18.) In every possible way Satan sought to prevent the execution of God's Plan of Redemption.

GOD'S REDEEMING ACHIEVEMENT – ONE DECISIVE ACT

We have already spoken of the manifestation of God's Love and Holiness in redeeming the human race as *one decisive act*. Let us examine this statement a little more closely. Would it not seem probable that if He undertook the settlement of the sin-question it would be completed in a single act, rather than to take the form of a process extending through centuries?

But the question might be asked, "How could He deal judicially with sinners of all ages and dispensations in a moment of time?" *Only by dealing with their Federal Head, whose representative acts they would individually ratify through their power of choice.* Therefore, after Jesus Christ, in His earthly walk, had manifested a dependent, holy, victorious life as the Last Adam, living in the sphere of Uncreated (Eternal) Life, He was ready to act representatively in connection with the race of the First Adam, with whom He had identified Himself. He, the Sinless One, who lived in the sphere of Life, Holiness, Peace, Love, voluntarily permitted His humanity to descend to the sin-poisoned atmosphere of the sphere in which the descendants of the First Adam dwelt. Personally, He was without sin. Representatively, the sin of the whole race was laid upon Him, and thus His humanity came within the operation of "the law of sin and death," which we have found to be absolutely inflexible. Representatively then, He must bear the stroke, the doom, the penalty that the sinful race deserved—that God's Holiness demanded.

It is evident that the sinlessness of the Sin-bearer magnifies the Holiness of God. Sinners deserved the stroke. The Sinless One did not; therefore, "the death of Jesus was a more splendid vindication of righteous rule than the death of all the sinners would have been" (Dr. Mabie, in *The Meaning and Message of the Cross*).

THE MODE OF CHRIST'S DEATH FORESHADOWED IN THE OLD TESTAMENT

Let us now consider the mode of this judgment-death. We find this stated in Acts 2:23: "Him, being delivered by the determinate counsel and foreknowledge of God, ye have taken and by wicked hands have *crucified* and slain." Was this mode of death indicated in the Old Testament Scriptures? The Passover lambs were offered on Jewish altars, but death by crucifixion is not a Jewish mode of putting to death. We know that at this time Rome was the proud mistress of the world and Palestine was under her domination; therefore God's Lamb was crucified upon a Roman Cross which all the world could see, figuratively speaking. Had He been put to death in earlier times, before the conquest of Rome or during the rule of the Maccabees, His death would have been less spectacular and would have made less outward impression. God had chosen a fitting time in the history of our race for the execution of His Redemptive Plan; therefore even the *mode* of Christ's death was such as most adequately met the requirements in connection with the execution of the same.

*Wonderfully the whole redemption story has been written in the starry sky. Long before the creation of man, the constellations spoke of the serpent, the virgin, the child, and, brighter than all, blazed the Cross in the Southern sky.

---

* *Note:* The teacher who would look into this subject would do well to obtain a copy of *The Gospel in the Stars* by Seiss.

It would seem that God gave many intimations of the Cross during the hundreds of years before the actual rugged beams were placed upon Calvary. Never did an Israelite prepare the Passover lamb without looking upon the cross formed by the wooden spits upon which the body of the lamb was placed before roasting. The longer of these extended vertically the length of the body; the shorter was placed horizontally from side to side. Startling indeed to our eyes would be the resemblance, although we cannot tell what impression was made upon the people of old.

We observe the form of the Cross in the arrangement of the furniture of the Tabernacle, while the serpent upon the pole also speaks of the Cross. (See Exo. 40:20-30; Num. 21:8-9.)

Psalm 22 is described by Dr. Scofield as a "graphic picture of death by crucifixion." Have the class read this psalm and note that every detail of Christ's crucifixion is described almost as perfectly as if the writer were an eyewitness of that scene, instead of writing hundreds of years before. Dr. Scofield adds, "When it is remembered that crucifixion was a Roman, not Jewish form of execution, the proof of inspiration is irresistible." We plainly see, then, that the Cross, as well as the Lamb, was foreshadowed in the Old Testament, which is entirely consistent with the foreknowledge of God mentioned in Acts 2:23.

THE CRUCIFIXION NARRATIVES

The class should now read the account of the Crucifixion as narrated in the four Gospels. Notice certain details in the account given by Matthew which are not found in the other narratives. Meditate upon the significance of these. Examine the words of Mark to see if they contain expressions not found elsewhere. Observe certain expressions in Luke's account that are characteristic of that Gospel, and find details in the Gospel of John that are omitted in all the others. Put these narratives together until the whole scene stands out vividly before the mind's eye. Arrange the various utterances of Christ upon the Cross in their order and meditate long and prayerfully upon their meaning. Have Isaiah 53:1-9 read and dwell carefully and reverently upon each phrase. As verse 6 is read let the teacher place a black disc with circular opening, over the star upon the cardboard symbol of "The God-Man." This opening should reveal the center of the star but must entirely cover the circles indicating "soul and body." (See Fig. 6.) Explain that sin could not be placed upon His essential Deity, but that His humanity was brought into the world for this very purpose. (See Heb. 2:9.) Call attention to the *all* in Isaiah 53:6. The sin of the entire race was laid upon Him, and for *our* transgressions "did the stroke fall on Him" (Rotherham translation). The proof of this is found in that awful cry, "My God, My God, why hast Thou forsaken Me?" Only a little while before those same lips had uttered the words, "Father, I know that Thou hast heard Me and that Thou hearest Me always" (John 11:41-42). The latter expression was natural to His sinless humanity, but now He is uttering the cry of a race of sinners separated from a holy God.

Truly "He who knew no sin was made sin for us" (2 Cor. 5:21). It was at this moment that He was *tasting death* for every man (see Heb. 2:9); and death, let us remember, is a "falling out of correspondence with environment." God was still His environment, but an awful something that He had never experienced before was pressing upon His human nature—a something that did not respond to God—a something that was causing untold agony—that something was the great mountain of human sin which was crushing His human soul.

THE VICARIOUS SUFFERING OF THE GOD-MAN

Can we understand this vicarious suffering of the God-Man? No, we can never fathom the mystery of that awful hour when God, in Christ, manifested His Suffering Love and Holiness. However, God has created us with a capacity for vicarious suffering upon a lower plane, that helps us to faintly appreciate this hour of agony.

Many a person has suffered for another, and in some persons the vicarious element is so strong that they seem to enter the very atmosphere of another's personality and actually *feel* that which another is experiencing. How often has this been true of a godly father or mother who has suffered agony over the wrongdoing of a wayward child? But such suffering even when most keen and sacrificial, fails in enabling us to understand the suffering of the Sinless One who actually *felt* the sin, not of a single personality, but of all the combined personalities of the human race. Notice that three times in Isaiah 53 we find the word *soul* used in connection with the suffering of the Redeemer. Read verses 10-12. We have previously found that the soul is the seat of self-consciousness. Very appropriate then, is its use in this passage—for His whole personality felt the awful shock of contact with sin. Psychologically He was experiencing the most terrible "complex." Sin, laid upon His sinless nature, caused a pouring out of His soul even unto death. He, whose constant expression of Love and Obedience had been "Lo, I come to do Thy Will," now felt laid upon His human soul that awful enmity to God, which was the sin of the human race. Impress upon the class that the vicarious suffering which brought us Redemption took place in the *inner man* of the human nature of our Lord.

But not only was the human soul of the God-Man crushed by the sin that He vicariously bore; He was also surrounded by all the hostile forces of Satan. This indeed was the "hour and power of darkness," of which He had spoken. (See Luke 22:53.) Satan and his host of fallen angels and demons compassed Him about. This was the strategic moment for Satan, and he put forth all the strength of his might against the Being upon the Cross, who hitherto had repulsed and overcome him, but who now hung as a sinner in the agony of separation from the face of God. "God hath forsaken Him, persecute and take Him," was truly the language of his heart.

This moment was the fulfilment of the prophecy uttered so long before concerning Satan—"Thou shalt crush His heel." Oh, the darkness of this hour! No wonder that the forces of nature responded to the awful conflict that was taking place in the invisible realm. (See Matt. 27:45.)

Suddenly a loud, triumphant cry comes from the Cross—"It is finished"; and then peacefully the words, "Father, into Thy hands I commend My spirit"—and it is all over.

The pious Jews who had delivered up their Messiah to be crucified were very anxious that He should not remain upon the Cross upon their especially holy Passover Sabbath. They scrupulously avoided profaning the Sabbath, and doubtless they also feared a reaction among the people if they were permitted to gaze upon the dying agonies of One whom many had reverenced, and whose benefactions they had received. Therefore knowing that death by crucifixion is a slow lingering process, the crucified often living many hours upon the Cross, they obtained permission of Pilate to have the legs of the three victims broken to hasten their death. Accordingly the soldiers proceeded to break the legs of "the first and of the other that was crucified with Him; but when they came to Jesus and saw that He was dead already, they brake not His legs" (John 19:31-33). Notice that this was a fulfillment of prophecy, and let us also observe that even this detail was foreshadowed in connection with each Passover lamb eaten by an Israelitish family. Great care was shown in serving the lamb, that not a bone should be broken. (See Num. 9:12; Psa. 34:20.) The soldiers were surprised to find Him dead already. This was something very unusual in one who was in the prime of young manhood. They could not account for His death, but that they might faithfully discharge their commands, "one of the soldiers with a spear pierced His side, and forthwith came there out blood and water." This is the testimony of an eyewitness, even John the beloved disciple, who seems to lay great stress upon this occurrence, for he adds concerning his testimony as a witness, "This testimony is true: and he knoweth that he saith true, that *ye might believe*." What is the value of this testimony? How does it establish the truth of the statement already made? A physician would be able to tell us. This death was caused by the actual rupture of the heart as a result of the awful agony that the God-Man experienced in being "made sin" for us.

THE PHYSICAL CAUSE OF THE DEATH OF JESUS

Dr. Wm. Stroud, in a very clear, scientific treatise upon the subject of the physical cause of the death of Jesus, after describing the heart and its functions, proceeds to portray the dilated condition of this organ resulting from powerful emotion. He adds, "In young and vigorous subjects the blood collected in the pericardium soon divides into its constituent parts, namely a pale watery liquid called serum, and a soft clotted substance of a deep red color termed crassamentum." Thus the statement "came there forth blood and water" indicates a ruptured heart; but there are other indications also. In the Gospel written by Luke, who was a physician, we read of the bloody sweat which indicates rupture of the heart caused by mental agony: "Being in an agony He prayed more earnestly; and His sweat was as it were great drops of blood falling down to the ground" (Luke 22:44). Other physicians have noted these statements and know that they clearly prove the physical cause of Jesus' death to be ruptured heart as the result of the most awful mortal agony, and at least one unbelieving physician, impressed by these physical proofs of Jesus' sin-bearing for the human race, was led to put faith in Him as his Redeemer.

In the light of this knowledge of the physical cause of Jesus' death, how increasingly sacred does the garden of Gethsemane scene become. There, the God-Man was beginning to enter the atmosphere of human sin, and as the agony became intense, He could feel the fatal distension of the heart, the coldness of the extremities, the difficult breathing—and He knew what these symptoms indicated. Still the agony increased and great drops of bloody perspiration fell to the ground and death seemed near; yet He must go to the Cross. He could not die in Gethsemane. His trust in God never wavered, "and there appeared unto Him an angel from heaven strengthening Him" (Luke 22:43). He calmly met the mob that came out to take Him, went through the weariness of the illegal trial, suffered indignities of various kinds, took up His heavy cross and turned toward the hill of Crucifixion. Oh, how our hearts go out to Him—"The Man of Calvary"—The Lamb of God!

THE BURIAL

The lifeless body is now taken down from the Cross and prepared for burial. Those tender eyes that had looked with compassion upon the multitude again and again during His earthly ministry and had beamed lovingly upon the little children surrounding Him, were now closed in death. Those hands that had touched the leper, the blind, the deaf, the dumb, the diseased, hang limply at His side as the body is lifted from the Cross. That voice that had stilled the waves, cast out demons, raised the dead, uttered words of Life and hope, is now still. He who a little while before had said, "I am the Resurrection and the Life," now lay quiet in death. Jesus was dead.

Then His body was placed in the tomb and a great stone was rolled to the door of the sepulcher (Matt. 27:57-60). Had Pilate cared to place an inscription upon the stone, he would have written, "Here lies Jesus, King of the Jews." Had Satan written the inscription, it would have read, "Here lies Jesus of Nazareth, whom I have overcome"; but if God had written the inscription, it would have been, *"Here lies the sinful human race."*

THE TWO ASPECTS OF CHRIST'S DEATH

The teacher will find it necessary again and again to call attention to the fact that what was true of Jesus Christ as our Representative is true of us. The two aspects of His death must clearly be seen if the members of the class are to possess an intelligent, adequate conception of God's Redemptive Plan. The truths of Redemption should never be presented in such a manner as to lead the hearers to feel that Christ died for them that they might not die; that He suffered for their sins that they might escape punishment. Rather should they be clearly shown that when the stroke fell on Him, they were executed; when He suffered death, they died in Him. This is the representative aspect as taught in the Bible. (See 2 Cor. 5:19 and Rom. 6:1-11.) The sinless Last Adam gathered the entire sinful race of the First Adam in His arms and took them to Calvary. The stroke fell upon Him and upon all whom He embraced; and, as *sinners,* the entire human race disappeared from the horizon of God's holiness.

A young Christian who had been meditating much upon the Redemptive work of Christ, found difficulty in perceiving how she, as a sinner, received what she deserved in Christ's dying for her. She believed the facts as stated in the written Word of God, but her sense of justice said, "I ought to be punished for my sin. It does not seem fair for another to be punished for what I have done." God very preciously gave her the illumination that she needed one night in a dream, in which she saw one whom she loved standing as a culprit before a stern, frowning figure representing Justice. The face of the wrongdoer wore a guilty, apprehensive look, as if the descending rod in the hand of Justice was about to administer a deserved yet fearful punishment. Just as the heavy rod was about to fall upon the extended hand of the culprit, the young woman herself, personifying love, rushed forward, and placing her upturned hand in the hand of the guilty one, caught the full force of the blow. The culprit's face revealed the consciousness of having received deserved punishment and at the same time it manifested true sorrow for the wrongdoing; a sorrow that was awakened by love's suffering interposition and substitutionary act. The young woman was then able to see that *she had been punished;* that personally, she received what she deserved as a sinner; but Christ had felt the force of the blow.

Here we see both identification and substitution. When we say, "Christ died for me," we refer to an element of His death that we could not share—(the *force* of the "stroke"): this is the Substitutionary Aspect of His death. When we say, "In Christ I died," we refer to the fact of our identification with Him in His death as our Representative.

THE DEATH THAT CHRIST "TASTED"

But now let us more seriously examine the substitutionary aspect of His death. What is meant by His "tasting death for every man?" (See Heb. 2:9.) Clearly this refers to something more than dissolution. What was this death? Let us again recall the definition of death as stated in our earlier lessons: "Death is a falling out of correspondence with environment." It is the logical result of sin. Sinners cannot respond to God. This inability to respond causes a *realized separation* from Him. We have found that, so far as man is concerned, this separation would be of everlasting duration. Everlasting separation from God would mean *everlasting death*. This was the death that Christ "tasted."

We see then very plainly that had He been the son of Joseph, and by a miracle the law of heredity had been set aside in order to render the child of *sinful* parents a *sinless* being, His benevolent attempt to become a sacrifice for the sin of His race would have involved Himself in this everlasting death; and it would not have effected any change in the status of the members of the race. Only a Being who possessed Uncreated Life could "taste" everlasting death without being held in its power. Only a Being who was under the "law of the Spirit of Life" could come within the sphere of the operation of "the law of sin and death" and render it inoperative by rising above it.

A very simple illustration will enable the class to grasp the meaning. An eagle is perched upon a crag overlooking a precipice. A serpent glides noiselessly towards the rock and fastens its coils upon the body of the bird. Both fall over the edge of the precipice, but before the bottom is reached, the eagle disentangles itself from the coils of the serpent and flies far up in the air, while the serpent falls to the earth below. The serpent is *controlled* by the force of gravity which draws it to the ground. The eagle feels the force of gravitation but overcomes it by the force of levitation.

The God-Man came into the world "with a death-bearing body and a Life-giving power" (Dr. Mabie); therefore, He could go down to the sphere of everlasting death, and rising above it in His Uncreated Life, He could take with Him those who should choose to go.

We are now able to perceive that something more than the death of Christ is needed to meet all the requirements of God's Plan of Redemption. The claims of God's holiness have been satisfied, but the claims of God's Love must also be met. God wants *sons*—beings who shall share His Life; therefore the Last Adam must be manifested as the Head of a new order or race of righteous, holy, glorified human beings. This transformation of sinful human beings would seem to be analogous to the reconstructive work of God as narrated in Genesis 1:2, and might be fittingly termed a "new creation." (See 2 Cor. 5:17.)

CHRIST'S RESURRECTION

Accordingly, upon the third day after the body of Jesus had been placed in the tomb, the stone was found rolled away. Christ had arisen. Oh, the glorious Resurrection Morn! What does it mean to us? The teacher should have the various passages recording this event read and compared. The first appearance of Christ after His Resurrection was to Mary Magdalene. (See John 20:14-18.) The second is mentioned in Matthew 28:9, and the other appearances are given in their order: third, Luke 24:15-32; fourth, Luke 24:34; 1 Corinthians 15:5; fifth, Luke 24:36-43; sixth, John 20:19-25; seventh, John 20:26-29; eighth, John 21; ninth, Matthew 26:32; 28:16; tenth, 1 Corinthians 15:6; eleventh, 1 Corinthians 15:7[a]; twelfth, 1 Corinthians 15:7[b]; thirteenth, Acts 1:9-11; fourteenth, 1 Corinthians 15:8. Study each reference and note the numbers and classes of persons who were witnesses. Also carefully notice what Christ says about His glorified body. Note wherein it differed from His body before the Crucifixion.

The Resurrection is said to be the best attested fact of the Gospel Record and this indicates its importance, for without the Resurrection, there would be no positive proof of the efficacy of His death. (See Rom. 4:25; 1 Cor. 15:12-21.)

In the Resurrected Christ we behold the same Personality that walked and taught in Galilee. Those tender, searching eyes beam as of old, yet with a new luster. Those nail-scarred hands are the same that ministered in blessing to the sick and needy, yet their earthiness has disappeared. The disciples gaze upon their glorified Lord in amazement and awe, yet He convinces them that He is the "very same Jesus." He permits them to handle Him; to examine the scars in His hands and the healed spear wound in His side (John 20:19-29). He eats before them (Luke 24:41-43); He enters into their daily needs and prepares their morning meal (John 21:1-14).

Can we understand this Resurrection power? No, for it belongs to God; but we shall experience it. The glorified body of our Lord shows us what our glorified bodies are to be. Not an atom is to be lost but *changed*. The teacher should now remove the black circle surrounding the star, and place over the white circles symbolizing spirit, soul and body, a gilt disc bearing similar circles and words. The star, denoting the Deity of the God-Man, is now seen over the gilt disc that symbolizes His glorified humanity. (See Fig. 7.)

CHRIST'S ASCENSION

Call attention to the fact that Christ remained forty days upon earth in His Resurrection body; then, after promising to send the "Comforter," *His Other Self*, to them, He ascended to heaven, from which He told them that He would return in visible form, and requested them to watch for His appearing. (See Acts 1:9-11.)

Up through the realm of the defeated enemy—Satan, the usurper—the God-Man passed in triumph, having shaken off from

Himself the hostile princes and rulers whom He "boldly displayed as His conquests, when by the Cross He triumphed over them" (Col. 2:15, Weymouth).

Up to "heaven itself," the third heaven, went the God-Man, and having fully executed God's Plan of Redemption, "He sat down at the right hand of God; from henceforth expecting, till His enemies be made His footstool" (Heb. 10:12-13).

God has corroborated the statement of Jesus upon the Cross—"It is finished," by the display of His Resurrection and Ascension Power. God's Plan of Redemption for the human race has been fully executed. Not a single thing remains to be done. Eternal Life and everlasting sonship are ready for any human being who chooses to accept the same.

There is not a being that's under the sun,
Nor above it, nor anywhere in the wide earth
 Nor in the whole heaven
 Not God nor Christ even;
Not all these combined can do aught, for 'tis Done!
 Done thoroughly, gloriously,
 Superbly, victoriously
 As God's Self would have it,
 Done! there we may leave it;
Christ's work on the Cross is of infinite worth
 Meeting sin in its root
 And through all its fruit;
And God rests; and Christ rests; and the man who believes
May rest as secure and established as They
And as happy, though heaven and earth pass away;
May rejoice to the full in the Life he receives.

Malachi Taylor

Part 3

GOD'S PLAN OF REDEMPTION APPROPRIATED AND MANIFESTED

Thus far our studies have been from the objective standpoint. We now consider the subjective aspect.

A word of caution is necessary in connection with this portion of our course. The teacher should not permit the class to take up these lessons until the truths presented in the first and second sections are really perceived. Frequent reviews are necessary that the teacher may be able to ascertain how much has been grasped by the individual members of the class, as all subjective teaching must rest upon a solid objective basis. If the objective is weak, the subjective will not be able to stand the strain of fierce, long continued temptation, or the subtle influence of error and fanaticism.

THE TERM "APPROPRIATION" EXPLAINED

Perhaps it will be well to explain the reason for the use of the word "appropriate" in this section. If we study the derivation of the verb *to appropriate,* we shall find that it indicates the act of taking something for one's own use. The mental picture is an outstretched hand receiving something that has been given, to be put to a certain definite use. It does not indicate self-effort beyond that of reaching forth the hand to receive a gift; therefore it seems a fitting word to use in reference to the extended hand of faith, receiving the Gift of God.

WHAT WE ARE TO APPROPRIATE

Now let us consider what we are to appropriate. In answering this question, we must again call attention to the representative aspect of Christ's Death and Resurrection. All that is included in His Death and Resurrection, with the exception of His substitutionary work, is true of all those who are identified with Him. In Him, we died to sin. We arose in Him, alive unto God. (See Rom. 6:1-11.) Those who share the Life of the Last Adam are to be conformed to His Image. Positionally, every redeemed human being arose when Christ arose; thus manifesting His victory over sin and death. Positionally, they ascended with Him; thus manifesting His victory over Satan and all the powers of darkness. God reckons upon this Representative aspect of Christ's death; therefore He speaks of the redeemed as if they were already experimentally what He knows they will be. In this connection read Ephesians 2:4-6 and Romans 8:28-30. Because God reckons upon what the Life of the Last Adam in a human being who has appropriated Him will accomplish, He can consistently say to one who is conscious of failure and weakness, "Thou art all fair, my love; there is no spot in thee." Someone has truly said—*God was the first being to put faith in Calvary.*

The teacher must lead the class to see that God does not have to wait for the historical manifestation of anything before He sees it. Notice that "He chose us in Him (Christ) before the foundation of the world that we should be holy and without blame before Him" (Eph. 1:4). He saw the redeemed, i.e., those who should appropriate the Life of the Redeemer, before He created the world, as plainly as when in a yet distant future the entire host of the redeemed, conformed to the glorified humanity of the Last Adam, will stand in His presence.

GOD'S UNIQUE CONSTITUTION OF BEING

We must remember that God has no past, no future. It is always present tense with Uncreated Life. God IS.

> God has His own unique constitution of Being. He is the Eternal God and therefore independent of all time—He is the "I AM," to whom past, present and future are equally *today,* who is alike without beginning and without end, without succession of days or change of condition. (Dr. A. T. Pierson)

In the light of the present day discussion of the theory of *relativity,* these statements seem perfectly logical and may be apprehended, although never comprehended. Concerning Creation and Redemption, we may say in the language of an old-time writer— "God speaks and it *is* done—thousands of years ago—but lately found out by me."

We are now able to perceive that we are to appropriate a measure of the *very same Life* that infills the glorified personality of the Lord Jesus Christ. This Life is the Uncreated Life of God, permeating a human personality. Have the class read 1 John 5:11 and then fasten a small gilt disc containing these words, upon the large disc symbolizing Uncreated Life. (See Fig. 8.) Explain that a human being can never have the Life of God except through the Eternal Son. Uncreated Light is stored in Him for us. Light existed before the sun, but in the account of God's Reconstructive Work as recorded in the first chapter of Genesis, we find that God prepared the sun to be a light-holder or container, that light might be diffused throughout the earthly atmosphere. Even so God prepared the Son—the Word—Christ Jesus, to be a Holder or Container of Uncreated Life and Light; "In Him was Life and the Life was the Light of men" (John 1:4). In this connection Christ said of Himself, "I am the Light of the world" (John 9:5). We now understand what God means when He says, "He that hath the Son hath the Life; and he that hath not the Son hath not the Life" (1 John 5:12);

"the Life," referring to His Life—Uncreated or Eternal Life, which He has stored for us in the Son.

THE ACTIVITIES OF THE HOLY SPIRIT IN CONNECTION WITH OUR APPROPRIATION

We now need to consider how we are to appropriate all that God has for us in Christ Jesus: In other words, how may these truths that we have considered objectively become ours experimentally?

We found in a previous lesson that the threefoldness of God is to be considered in connection with every act of God. We commonly speak of the three "persons" of the Trinity, for lack of a better expression; but this is misleading unless we are careful to remember that the Trinity is One Personality. We should never separate the threefoldness of God, but always think of Him as the *One God,* visualized in Christ, but also invisibly active in the Holy Spirit.

For the purpose of clear thinking, we will now speak of the activities of God the Holy Spirit in enabling sinful human beings to perceive and appropriate the Redemptive Work planned by God the Father and executed by God the Son. The Holy Spirit's *method,* if we may use that word, is the same at each crisis of appropriation. There is always the "brooding process," followed by man's perception of need; then there is illumination concerning God's Plan of Redemption executed at Calvary, to meet the need. This is followed by the quickening of faith in the needy one, and then the will is energized so that the choice may be made. The word "brooding" referred to, is suggested by the verb in the last phrase of Genesis 1:2. "The Spirit of God, i.e., God, the Holy Spirit, moved (Heb. *brooded*) upon the face of the waters." Pastor Stockmayer in his *Meditations in Genesis* shows the analogy between the work of the Holy Spirit in connection with the reconstruction of the chaotic earth and His work in the ruined sinner. Concerning this preparatory work he says, "The Spirit of God prepares the way for the

Word of God." Before God speaks the word (vv. 3, 6, 9, 14, 20, 24, 26), the Spirit of God must make ready His way. He hovers, He moves, He broods over that mass as a hen broods over her eggs. Before the sinner wakes up to grace out of the world of chaos in which he has been living, an uneasiness comes over him. It is the Holy Spirit brooding over him. Theologians name this "predestinating grace." The teacher should explain that this preparatory work must be accomplished in those for whom we are praying. While we are praying and giving forth the Word of God in public assemblies or in personal conversation, the Holy Spirit is using our words and our intercession to bring about the *uneasiness* and sense of need that develops into what is theologically termed "conviction." A convicted sinner must always be shown Calvary as meeting his need, and this the Holy Spirit proceeds to do— revealing a crucified Savior whose sin-bearing has made it possible for the sinner to pass from the sphere of sin into that of Eternal Life. Faith is so quickened that the Redemptive Work of Calvary seems no longer an historical event for sinners in general, but the sinner exclaims, "He died for *me.*" There is penitence and in some cases much emotion is manifested, but not until the energized will chooses to pass from the sphere of sin into that of Eternal Life, is the person truly regenerated. This act of the will is called *repentance.* It is a "right about face movement."

REPENTANCE AN ACT OF THE WILL

It cannot be too strongly emphasized that repentance is an act of the will. In its beginning there may be no sense of gladness or reconciliation to God; but just the consciousness that certain ways of life are wrong, mistaken, hurtful and grieving to God; and the desire, which becomes the determination to turn from them, to seek Him who formed the mountains and created the wind, that maketh the morning darkness and treadeth upon the high places of the earth.

Repentance may be accounted the other side of faith. They are the two sides of the same coin; the two aspects of the same act. For purpose of clear thinking it is well to discriminate in our use of the words repentance and penitence, using the former of the first act of the will, when, energized and quickened by the Spirit of God, it turns from dead works to serve the living and true God; and the latter, of the emotions which are powerfully wrought upon as the years pass by the Spirit's presentation of all the pain and grief which our sin has caused, and is causing to our blessed Lord. *We repent once,* but are *penitents always.* We repent in the will; we are penitent in the heart. (Rev. F. B. Meyer)

If the nature of repentance were better understood, Christians would not be troubled over certain passages of Scripture that are often quoted to prove that a child of God may lose Eternal Life: e.g., Hebrews 6:6. The teacher must dwell upon this subject sufficiently to enable the class to clearly perceive the difference between repentance and penitence. They must see that in the very nature of things, repentance, as has been defined, is an act that can never be repeated. The class will be helped to perceive this, if the teacher will exhibit a fifth piece of cardboard, uniform in size with the other four, but placed horizontally, instead of vertically, containing a cross in the center and at the left of the cross a black disc, above which should be placed the words "Sphere of Sin and Death." At the right of the Cross a gilt disc should be placed, above which are the words "Sphere of Eternal Life in Christ Jesus." (See Fig. 9.)

Proceed to show that when the sinner, who is within the sphere of sin and death, chooses to leave that sphere and enter the sphere of Eternal Life in Christ Jesus, he actually passes experimentally from one to the other; the cross standing as a gate which opens at his touch of faith to let him through, but which closes behind him and can never be opened upon the Life Side of the Cross to permit his return.

The members of the class must be able to perceive very, very clearly that when the choice is made, a measure of Eternal Life, God's own Uncreated Life, comes into the spirit of man. He is now truly regenerated; i.e., *born again*. Let the class become familiar with the following definition of regeneration.

REGENERATION
A BIRTH RELATIONSHIP WITH GOD

Regeneration is a birth relationship with God, instantaneous and indissoluble. At this point, place a small gilt disc in the center of the black disc symbolizing the sin-stained "spirit," "soul," "body," and call for John 1:12 and 1 John 3:1-3 to be read by the class. (See Fig. 10.) It is evident that a birth relationship can never be dissolved. A child may disobey its father's commands, may grieve his heart and wander away from him, but he is still his father's child. Other relationships may cease. A business partnership may be dissolved; the marriage relation may be annulled; friends may be separated, but birth relationship is indissoluble.

Unless the members of the class really see the meaning of this birth relationship with God, progress in the Christian life will be slow and uncertain. Many persons seem to think that they remain Christians while they are not consciously disobeying God's commands, but should they do something that they consider wrong, they think that they have fallen from grace and have lost Eternal Life. Could Christians but remember that the life they receive at regeneration is Uncreated Life—*God's Life that can never change*, and that He calls them His own children, they would cease to permit their fluctuating emotions to determine their standing before God. When a sinner is willing to admit his sinful, lost condition, and definitely turns to God from sin—appropriating the Life of God in Christ Jesus—that very instant he becomes a child of God, and through all Eternity will be a Child of God; for he is put within the sphere of Eternal Life; therefore he now possesses in his spirit a Life that will remain there as long as God lives. (See John 1:12; Rom. 8:16-17.) This is what regeneration means. He is also justified. (See Rom. 8:30.)

JUSTIFICATION DEFINED AND ILLUSTRATED

The class should learn the meaning of Justification, which is—*a new standing before God.* Before his new birth his standing was that of a sinner; now it is that of a child of God—in New Testament terms, a "saint." An illustration may help the class to perceive that justification does not depend upon our righteous acts but upon our attitude toward God. It is the result of our choice, not the reward for our good works. In Tennyson's poem, *The Beggar Maid,* we find that king Cophetua made the barefooted beggar girl in poor attire, his queen. Her standing before her marriage to the king was that of a poor beggar maid; upon her marriage she was at once a queen. Her change of status depended solely upon her choosing to become the bride of a king. After her marriage, she might put on clothing befitting her position and adorn herself with the jewels that the king should bestow, but her change of status would not depend upon such acts; indeed the changed clothing would be the result of her previously changed status. The person who one moment says, "I am a poor lost sinner" may the next moment sing, "I'm the child of a King."

THE SPHERE OF THE BELIEVER

Most carefully should the nature of redeeming grace be presented to the class. Grace is unmerited favor bestowed by God upon repentant human beings, but it is favor that He longs to bestow. Have the following passages read: Ephesians 2:4-10; Romans 5:15, 21; 3:23-24 and find similar passages.

Regeneration marks the first crisis of appropriation in the life of a Christian. A new life-principle has entered the spirit of the believer, and his personality is in a new sphere. He is "in Christ Jesus," and Christ's Life is in him, and his condition is absolutely unalterable. To think otherwise would be to doubt the unchanging nature of the Life that enspheres him. In connection with the use of the word "sphere," the following quotation from Dr. A. T. Pierson will be helpful:

A circle surrounds us, but only on one plane; but a sphere encompasses, envelops us, surrounding us in every direction. If you draw a circle on the floor, and step within its circumference you are within it only on the level of the floor. But, if that circle could become a sphere, and you within it, it would on every side surround you—above and below, on the right hand and on the left. Moreover, the sphere that *surrounds* you also *separates* you from whatever is outside of it. Again, in proportion as such a sphere is strong it also *protects* whatever is within it from all that is without—from all external foes or perils. And yet again, it *supplies,* to whomsoever is within it whatever it contains. This may help us to understand the great truth taught with such clearness especially in the New Testament. Christ is there presented throughout as the sphere of the believer's whole life and being, and in this truth are included these conditions: First, Christ Jesus surrounds or embraces the believer in His own life; second, He separates the believer in Himself from all hostile influences; third, He protects him in Himself from all perils and foes of his life; fourth, He provides and supplies in Himself all that is needful.

These two expressions, "In Christ Jesus" and "Christ in you," or their equivalents, indicate the whole gospel story. We find them used very many times in the epistles. It will be well for the class to find some of these expressions for themselves. Notice how they abound in the first chapter of the epistle to the Ephesians.

GOD'S ULTIMATE PURPOSE CONCERNING THE REGENERATED

The teacher will now need to call attention to God's ultimate purpose concerning the life of the regenerated one. We have already seen that God marked out the redeemed before the founding of the world to be conformed to the Image of His Son. And we have further seen that He had in mind the glorified Last Adam, when He created the first Adam; therefore God's purpose for His redeemed one is that he shall become like *The Man in the Glory.*

CONFORMITY TO TYPE

We know full well that life on any plane, if unhindered, will become conformed to its type. In other words, it will ultimately manifest all the characteristic qualities of the individual life-principle. The teacher will explain, if necessary, the various definitions of the word *type,* that the class may not become confused with its double use in Bible Study. This law of conformity to type may be illustrated as follows. Notwithstanding the fact that vegetable life presents almost endless variety in order, group and family, yet in the original germ no difference is discernible. An invisible life-principle within each germ fashions the particular form of vegetable life that the Creator designs. Thus the original germ of the oak and the lily look exactly alike. Examined through the microscope, no difference whatever is to be seen; yet the oak life is within one germ, and the lily life within the other, and these two widely differing forms of life are developed according to the individual life-principle.

The same is true of animal life. In the original germs no difference is discernable, yet the individual life-principle in one germ fashions an animal to live upon the land, while that in another germ forms an animal to live in the water or to fly in the air.

And not only does the individual life-principle fashion its special form of life, but if conditions for growth are fulfilled, it will cause the life to become fully conformed to its type. To illustrate: The lily life is in the tiny green shoot appearing above the ground but it is not conformed to its type. It has not yet manifested all the characteristic qualities of the lily life. However, there comes a day when the beautiful lily life is fully manifested in the lovely, fragrant blossoms that crown its glossy, green stalk. It is now conformed to type.

God, the Creator, has made provision for each variety of life to conform to its type. It makes no difference whether it be upon the plane of vegetable, animal or human life; if conditions are fulfilled, conformity is certain. We will now consider the nature of these conditions upon each plane of life.

Vegetable life is simple, unconscious life; therefore the response to God's provision for growth and ultimate conformity to type will be unconscious, spontaneous. The lily simply bathes in the sunshine, drinks in the rain and the dew, and absorbs from the soil that which it needs. This response to God's provision for its conformity is beautifully set forth in Luke 12:27.

Animal life is conscious life, although not self-conscious life; therefore the response to the provision for growth is of a different kind. We see this indicated in Psalm 104:21 and Luke 12:24. God provides animals with food, but they have to "gather" it. Unlike the lily, they are created with organs of locomotion, and they must use them if they are to attain maturity of growth.

In considering the conditions for growth on the plane of human life, which is self-conscious life, we find that as human beings are created with the power of choice, and intellectual and moral faculties in addition to bodily powers, the response to God's provision will be of a higher order than that of the animal creation. Man has to use all of his powers if his conformity to type morally, intellectually, and physically is to be realized; yet he cannot by self-effort add "one cubit to his stature." He simply uses his God-given power of choice in such a manner that the life-principle within succeeds in causing conformity to type.

We must now see how this law of conformity to type is manifested on the higher plane of regenerated human life. We must remember that a new life-principle has been introduced into the human spirit. There is not a single spark of Uncreated, or Eternal Life, in a human being until the instant of regeneration. This fact has already been set forth in the first section of these studies, but the teacher needs to constantly keep it before the class, as so many persons have mistaken ideas in reference to this subject. We must also recall the fact that biology says, "Life on one plane cannot generate life on a higher plane; but, if the life on one plane were ever to know life on a higher plane, there must be a *prepared organism to receive* such a life, and *a prepared medium of transmission from the higher plane to the lower,* so that the new life may be received as *an immediate, instantaneous bestowal."* The agreement between this statement and God's written Word is perfect. The God-Man is the prepared medium of transmission, and every human being is a "prepared organism" for the reception of life on a higher plane—because of the created spirit, as a capacity for this life, and the created power to choose it. If the will has made its choice, then this new Life-principle will fashion within the human personality that "new creature" mentioned in 2 Corinthians 5:17. And, if the conditions for growth are fulfilled, then conformity to the Type—the Glorified God-Man—will be realized.

CONDITIONS FOR THE CHRISTIAN'S CONFORMITY TO TYPE

What are the conditions? These: Complete dedication of the entire personality to God, and continual reckoning upon His working within, both to "will and to do of His good pleasure"; thus transforming from "one degree of glory to another," until Christ shall be *fully formed* within the personality. (See Phil. 2:13; 2 Cor. 3:18; Gal. 4:19.)

ENTIRE DEDICATION MARKS THE SECOND CRISIS OF APPROPRIATION

This dedication marks a second definite crisis in the life of the believer, but too often the subject is ignored by Christian workers, or presented in such a manner as to cause confusion and to lead into fanaticism. The teacher who has faithfully followed this course thus far will have little difficulty in leading the class to see the absolute necessity of a definite handing over of the whole being to God for His transforming work. It is the only logical thing to do, for God cannot fill a personality with the "Life of the Lamb" against the will of the person; and if the personality continues to manifest the life of the old Adam, he will not be a *son brought to glory.*

We have seen that God's Plan of Redemption was settled judicially and decisively at Calvary, but if Christians are not enabled to become conformed to the Image of Christ, it cannot be said to have been settled effectually. Christ's vicarious suffering for the members of the human race would not cause a realization of God's Eternal Purpose for them, unless they were thereby enabled to partake of His Life and become conformed to His Image. The members of the human race must come into such a union with Him, that His death should be their death, and His Life their Life. "When Christ is said to die for another, it is upon the presupposition that such a one, a real believer, is to come into mystical, vital union with Christ; so that as thus identified with Christ, the believer dies with Christ to the life of self and sin, and then lives again in the power of a risen life" (from *The Meaning and Message of the Cross*). It is to be feared that many Christians see only the substitutionary aspect of Christ's death, and their lives express what their lips would hardly dare to say—"Christ died for me; therefore I can live as I please."

We have spoken of the Holy Spirit's "method" of working at each crisis of appropriation. We noted the "brooding" until a sense of need is awakened, then the vision of Calvary as meeting the need, [then] the quickening of faith and energizing of the will before the choice of the individual is made; and we find this to be true in the case of the Christian who is led from Regeneration to Sanctification.

TWOFOLD ASPECT OF SANCTIFICATION

It will be observed that Sanctification includes the act of *dedication*, which is *instantaneous*, and *transformation*, which is a *process*, never ending until Glorification is realized. With this in mind, let us follow the working of the Holy Spirit at this crisis.

The regenerated one has begun to see that a life of victory is impossible; old habits assert themselves much to the grief of the person; resolutions are made but prove ineffectual in the hour of temptation. The condition of the believer is well described in Romans 7:22-24. The Holy Spirit has succeeded in causing a realization of need; now He whispers, "Look again to Calvary. See, not only did Christ suffer for your sins, but He took you with Him to the Cross. Your old self was nailed there with Him; with Him it was laid in the tomb, and *that was its termination; for only the Life of Christ arose.* Will you let His risen, victorious Life be lived out in your personality?" There is hesitation for a time as visions of possible future suffering and loss are presented to the mind, but the yearning love of Christ conquers, and then the irrevocable, inclusive YES is said. From the depths of the being comes the

> Yes, Lord,
> One great Eternal yes
> To all my Lord shall say;
> To all I know or yet shall know
> Of all the untried way.

This is a blessed moment in the life of a child of God, for now the Holy Spirit is free to enter upon the transforming work which will eventually cause complete conformation to the Image of Christ.

FIRST AND SECOND CRISIS OF APPROPRIATION CONTRASTED

The following quotation illustrates the difference between the first and second crisis of appropriation.

Is not the failure in connection with the realization of experimental victory over sin, due to the fact that we have not perceived the need of definitely appropriating our individual infilling with the Anointing of the Holy Spirit which was poured upon Christ our Head, and which was to include each member of His body? It is true that we have a measure of the Holy Spirit when we are regenerated, for one cannot be "born again" without the Spirit of God; but that is not knowing Him in His fullness. A simple illustration may help us to see this: Suppose we see a stretch of marshy land full of pools of stagnant water, emitting noisome odors and vapors. Right above it is a beautiful lake, full of clear, sparkling water. As we look at this beautiful water, we think of the transformation which would be realized if it could flow over the waste land below; but a dam of solid masonry effectually prevents this. However, one day as we pass by we discover that the flashboard of the dam has been raised, and now a stream of the clear, life-giving water is flowing over the marshy land below. Already a great change has been effected, but there still remain unsightly, muddy pools on either side of the stream of pure water, and involuntarily we exclaim, "Oh, if the water would come down and flood all this place, how beautiful it would then appear." A little later, we pass by again, and lo, what a transformation! Someone has raised the floodgate of the dam and the water is pouring down, rapidly covering the entire stretch of marshy land, until all the muddy pools of stagnant water are covered and all that we can see is the pure, sparkling water of the lake. When we are "born again" (regenerated), it is like the raising of the flashboard. The Life of God through the Holy Spirit comes into our spirit, making us indeed new creatures in Christ Jesus; but oh, what a circumference of our being remains practically untouched by this Life. When we definitely yield to the infilling and control of the Holy Spirit, saying to Him, "I choose to let Thee transform me to the Image of Christ, at any cost," then we realize that the Eternal Spirit is manifesting Himself within our being in a new way, which may be likened to the opening of the floodgate. (from *Identification*)

To symbolize the results of this second crisis of appropriation, the teacher may place over the small gilt disc which has been fastened to the black disc containing the three circles "spirit," "soul," "body," a slightly larger gilt disc with eight (or more) rays extending in various directions, the points barely touching the circle symbolizing the *body*. (See Fig. 11.) A still larger symbol, of the same shape, may be added later to illustrate the progressive stages of Transformation, if desired. And if a gilt disc containing the three circles symbolizing spirit, soul and body, could be held over this partly covered black disc, it would symbolize the future Glorification of the believer. (See Fig. 12.)

SUGGESTIONS AND WARNINGS IN CONNECTION WITH THE SECOND CRISIS OF APPROPRIATION

So much unwise teaching has been given concerning the external manifestations following this crisis that frequently Christians are led to expect a great display of the Supernatural at this time, and in many cases honest souls become greatly confused. One who has seen much fanaticism and suffering as the result of such teaching has written the following suggestions which may be helpful to the members of the class:

> It matters little what outward manifestations may accompany the sweeping of God's Presence through "all the rooms of the house," or whether there is any manifestation at all. The redeemed one simply *knows* that "The Lord is in His Holy Temple," and that henceforth He will cleanse and purify and manifest Himself *as He chooses*....This second definite step is called by various names according to the individual perspective of the various teachers. Some call it the "Second Blessing"; others, the "Blessing of Sanctification"; while others speak of it as the "Baptism of the Holy Spirit"; and it is also set forth as the "Blessing of a Clean Heart," "Perfect Love," "The Anointing," "Pentecost," etc. While all these terms are in a measure descriptive of this second plane of appropriation of Christ's Redemptive Work, perhaps no one term adequately expresses all the truth concerning the same; therefore, it is unwise to insist dogmatically upon the acceptance of any particular term as essential to the truth which the Holy Spirit reveals at this stage of the Christian life. Great simplicity in teaching is needed, lest in

our presentation of the truth concerning this experience, unconsciously we permit the *naming* of the experience to become more prominent than the experience itself. *Not the naming, but the yielding, is the essential thing.* If the regenerated person has intelligently, definitely, irrevocably, yielded to the complete control of the Holy Spirit, he is thereafter identified with Christ in *His Anointing*—His Fullness of the Holy Spirit; and as a result, he will be led step by step into the experimental knowledge of the Cross of Calvary and the power of the Resurrection Life.

While the *inward* results of abandonment to the control of the Holy Spirit are the same in all persons, the outward manifestations vary according to temperament and training. The immediate results outwardly need to be carefully watched, as the temptations of Satan are very subtle at this point. In nearly all cases, the emotions, whose duty it is to send telegrams back and forth between the "inner" and the "outer" man, are quickly affected by the new order of things, and before the intellect can clearly act, the body is called upon to give expression to the demands of the emotions. It is owing to this fact that we see many persons manifesting their joy by singing, praising God, clapping of hands, etc., while in others we see the cessation of usual bodily movements and great stillness of the whole being, while the countenance expresses holy awe and worship. These manifestations, and others which might be named, are legitimate and should not be criticized or checked; but sometimes manifestations are to be seen which are not natural but are the result of supernatural power of an evil kind. Satan seeks to imitate the Holy Spirit and to produce manifestations which he would have the person believe to be of God. This is for the purpose of causing confusion in the mind of the Christian so that the work of transformation may be hindered and the conduct of the Christian may become such as will bring the truth into discredit and disrepute.

There is great need of quiet listening to God's voice in the depth of the being and a *knowledge of God's Written Word when the emotions are unusually excited.* Remember that the Holy Spirit, who inspired the words, "Let all things be done decently and in order," never leads one to do what is unseemly or unnecessary. Bearing this in mind, we should test the physical manifestations which we experience, or see in others. As a result, we may find that many manifestations which we thought to be of the Holy Spirit are of a psychical nature, and thus instead of proving our exalted spiritual condition, they indicate our lack of complete yieldedness in the circumference of our being. And if through wilfulness we permit these manifestations to continue, we may open the door to evil spirits who will cause manifestations which will produce most disastrous results.

As the Holy Spirit sheds light upon these manifestations, we are led to see that undue shaking or jerking of the body, long continued prostrations of the body, and other manifestations that might be named, always indicate that the true, deep Life of God, the Holy Spirit, has not permeated the entire circumference of the being. Normal prostration, that is, prostration which contains no element of the abnormal or evil supernatural, comes to a great sinner as the result of conviction of sin, or to worthy saints in consequence of great revelations, but it is *not long continued.* As examples under the latter head, we read of Daniel, Ezekiel, John. If we bear in mind that the Holy Spirit enters the spirit of man, then permeates and controls his powers of soul, and then brings his bodily powers into subjection, so that the entire being is experimentally at God's disposal, we shall be able to understand that unnecessary outward manifestations indicate fanatical or immature Christians. The ripe saint is the quiet, well poised, Spirit-controlled person.

INWARD RESULTS OF ABANDONMENT TO THE HOLY SPIRIT

We now need to note the inward results of the Abandonment to the Holy Spirit. First: *Christ is more real.* The Holy Spirit does not speak of Himself. He does not call attention to Himself. He always glorifies Christ (John 16:14). Notice that the striking feature of the work of the Holy Spirit in the early apostolic church was this: He caused the believers of that time to *realize their identification with a crucified, risen, ascended, glorified Lord.* All else—signs and wonders, miracles and gifts, were but incidental to such identification. Indeed, without the realization of their identification with their Lord, all these outward incidentals would have proven exceedingly harmful to the early church.

Second: *There is a new light upon God's Written Word.* The Bible indeed becomes a new Book. It is regarded as the very *Spirit-breathed Word of God* and to be treated with as much respect and reverence as if uttered by the audible voice of the Lord, and is to be perfectly obeyed. The veil seems lifted from obscure passages and Christ stands revealed in new beauty and glory. Especially is the work of Christ as the Redeemer illumined and glorified. (See John 16:15.)

Third: *There begins to be realized experimental victory over sin.* The Christian perceives that the death that Christ died as our Representative was a "death *unto* sin" (Rom. 6:10), and that he is identified with Christ in *this death;* also that as Christ arose to a sphere wherein sin does not exist, but where Righteousness reigns, even so he is identified with Christ in *this new life;* and as a result of his "reckoning" (or acting) upon this truth, he realizes victory in his daily life, through the indwelling Holy Spirit who corroborates what God says, as he reckons upon it.

Fourth: *The Love of God is manifested in the daily life in self-sacrifice for others.* Service for God now proceeds from love, rather than from duty. The language of the heart is, "I *want* to do this" instead of "I *must* do it."

Fifth: *Increasing light upon God's dispensational plan,* especially the prophecies concerning the Coming of Christ for His saints, and His coming with them in the outward manifestation of His kingdom in this world. The Christian begins to live in the light of Christ's Return. It is more than theory with him. It is a constant, bright anticipation and expectation. "He shall show you things to come" (John 16:13).

Sixth: The Christian perceives that as a result of his identification with Christ in His risen, glorified Life, he *may realize* a *foretaste* of the *Resurrection power* which will eventually change his body in the "twinkling of an eye" at translation. This foretaste, or "earnest" (see 2 Cor. 5:4-5), is indicated in Romans 8:11 as the quickening of the mortal body by the indwelling Holy Spirit moment by moment, enabling the believer to finish the work given him to do. Notice that it is the *mortal* body, not a dead body, that is to be thus quickened. This quickening of the mortal body does not refer to the final act of translation. At translation the mortal body is *changed* (see 1 Cor. 15:52), but *this quickening is an every day experience.*

Seventh: *There is power in prayer and service* because the believer is reckoning upon his identification with Christ who has "all power."

REVELATION OF THE SOULISH LIFE

The teacher must lead the class to see that this new experience is not the ultimate as many seem to think. It is rather the beginning of practical transformation, which will proceed from stage to stage as the Holy Spirit takes the believer down into an ever deepening realization of his identification with Christ in His death, not to sin alone, but to the natural or soulish life as well. So much of the activity of Christians is of a soulish nature, that a truly spiritual person is rarely seen, and when seen is not understood. All Christians are *in* Christ, and many desire to live *for* Christ; but it is quite another matter to have the daily life, a manifestation *of* Christ. Paul could truly say, "to me to live is Christ," but how many Christians are able to say the same?

The God-Man in His earthly life had no sin in Him, yet He constantly refused to let His human emotions or affections shape His ministry; nor would He be led by His own unsullied intellect apart from the revealed will of God. He was the most dependent Being ever born into this world; therefore everything in His life was *of God.*

He permitted Lazarus to die and the loving, trusting faith of Mary and Martha to be sorely tried, rather than to let His tender, compassionate heart cause Him to go to Bethany before His Father's time.

One of the secondary evidences of the Holy Spirit's control of the believer is this illumination concerning the soulish life. If the members of the class are shown that this perception of soulishness is a mark of normal Christian growth, they will not be overwhelmed when the depths of the self-life are revealed; nor will they be inclined to boast of their "holiness" or "absolute perfection." Remember that the ripest saint is the one who is most dependent.

TRANSFORMATION A PROCESS

Emphasize the fact that the act of dedication, like the new birth, is instantaneous, but transformation is a process; also, that "being filled with the Holy Spirit," an expression found in the New Testament and often quoted by earnest Christians, does not denote a finality. It is rather an indication of the controlling Power who is filling the personality of the believer. One familiar with New Testament Greek would easily discover that the tense used forbids the thought of the personality being filled once for all with the Holy Spirit, so that no more of His presence might enter. The word picture is that of a pipe connected with a never failing spring, through which the water is constantly flowing, rather than that of a bottle full of water but tightly corked.

Nowhere in the Scriptures is there promised a personal filling with the Spirit which shall be in any sense final; and it is only as a crisis of appropriation which leads to a daily process of renewal, that we are called to be filled." (Rev. J. Stuart Holden, in *The Price of Power*)

Therefore we see that the normal daily life of a yielded Christian may be described as

A moment by moment faith in a moment by moment Savior, for a moment by moment cleansing, and a moment by moment filling. As I trust Him, He fills me; so long as I trust Him, He fills me. The moment I begin to believe, that moment I begin to receive; and so long as I keep believing, praise the Lord, so long I keep receiving. (Rev. Charles Inwood)

VICTORY OVER SATAN

Another subject must now be introduced. Not only must the believer manifest his identification with Christ in His death to sin, and his freedom from the dominion of the self-life; but he must also manifest His victory over Satan. Many Christians fail at this point because they do not plainly see that the victory over Satan really has been won. They speak of this victory in the future tense instead of the past; therefore the teacher must again refer to the significance of Christ's Ascension, which proves that He had previously overcome the entire force of evil, ere He passed through the aerial region of Satan and "sat down," with the majestic calmness of a mighty Conqueror, at God's right hand. Have the class read Ephesians 1:20-23; Colossians 2:15; Hebrews 2:14; 1 John 3:8 again and again, until the *crushed head of the serpent* is plainly seen. Pray that they may see this and realize the sense of freedom and victory that comes as a result.

Well has Andrew Murray expressed the truth, when he says, "In the invisible world the Cross is the symbol of victory." The fact that God's Word declares that Christ has overcome Satan and made of him and his evil host "an open show" proves the possibility of victory, for the Christian identified with the Victorious Lord, over all the power of the enemy.

Although utterly defeated, Satan has sought to keep human beings in ignorance of his defeat, that he may still hold them in his power. As the Holy Spirit reveals the triumph of Christ and the believer sees his identification with the Victor of Calvary, he passes beyond the reach of the defeated one into that place where "the wicked one toucheth him not." (See 1 John 5:18.) Henceforth he regards Satan as a defeated foe, and united with the Conqueror and in utter dependence upon Him, he uses His authority over all the power of the defeated enemy. (See Luke 10:19.) Encourage the class to speak of Satan as *the defeated one*. This simple expression conveys to the evil intelligences the fact that the one using it has found out the truth concerning the Victory of Calvary and is identified with the Victor.

It will be well for the teacher to lead the class to a better understanding of the condition of the invisible but real world of spirits, so far as the Bible throws light upon the same.

We must remember that Satan is not omnipotent, omniscient, nor omnipresent, since these are attributes of Deity alone. He would like to have us think that he possesses the attributes of Deity, and many Christians speak as if they considered this to be the case. He is commonly spoken of as if he were everywhere; by a figure of speech using his name for his emissaries, as a general's name is used to indicate the army under his command. And Satan is like a general in this respect—he has hosts, varying in rank and power under his command, who execute his carefully laid plans of warfare. Thus we read in Ephesians 6:10-18 of principalities, powers, world-rulers and wicked spirits under his command, arrayed against the people of God. We also find the armor of the Christian described. As we carefully study this passage we find that the Christian who is appropriating the life of Christ moment by moment, and who is believing the Word of God in regard to His victory over Satan, is "more than conqueror" in every conflict.

The following quotation may be of help to the teacher at this point:

> The redeemed one who has been shown the truth of Christ's Complete Victory over Satan, and of his own complete identification with his Victorious Lord, knows that he is in a place of safety. He rests upon the fact that his life is *hid with Christ in God;* therefore the wicked one toucheth him not. With Satan as a personality, he has but one thing to do, and that is to reckon upon the fact of his identification with his Ascended Lord sitting in the calmness of assured victory. This attitude of victory and unceasing prayer in the Spirit also powerfully affects the aerial messengers of the defeated one, those mighty fallen angels who seem to exercise especial power over the nations or localities respectively assigned them. See Daniel 10, particularly verses 13, 20-21, where two of these princes of Satan are named—the Prince of Persia and the Prince of Greece. Michael, one of God's angels, is also mentioned. (Read this chapter and the preceding chapter to see more clearly the relation between the prayers of God's people and this aerial activity.)
>
> Although direct combat with these aerial messengers of Satan is entrusted to God's aerial messengers, the holy angels, rather than to redeemed human beings, yet to us is given authority over demons, to be exercised at the leading of the Holy Spirit.

The fact that evil spirits (or demons) are exerting such tremendous influence upon persons at the present time should cause all earnest Christians to desire all the light that God has given concerning the way to keep clear of their ensnaring, and also the knowledge necessary to be used in delivering those who have become bound.

WHO ARE DEMONS?

The question may be asked, "Who are demons?" A close study of the cases of demonized persons described in the New Testament would preclude the idea that they are of the angelic order of created beings; moreover, the word for demon is *daimon,* instead of *angelos,* which is the word for angel. The early church fathers believed demons to be the wicked dead (human beings) and that belief is shared by many Christians of modern times. Says Dr. Haldeman in his recent book, *Can the Dead Communicate with the Living?,* "Scripture teaches us that a certain class of the dead do come back, enter in and possess the bodies of the living. These are called 'devils,' but the word should be 'demons.'"

The teacher will certainly be guilty of the omission of vital truth for the crisis days in which we are living, if the subject of demon possession is passed by. The members of the class should be carefully instructed as to the way in which persons may unwittingly give ground to demons. They should see that a perception of their identification with the Victor of Calvary is *absolutely necessary* if they are to constantly and victoriously resist the obsession of evil spirits. They should be taught that manifesting a spirit of self-pity, pride, jealousy, discouragement, inordinate affection, may give just the ground that is necessary for the *manipulation* of evil spirits, if not full possession.

Entertaining fanatical religious views always opens the door to evil spirits, as truly as does any wrong practice. The fact that Christian workers, missionaries and other devoted children of God have suffered greatly from the manipulation of evil spirits during the last few years, proves that the necessary teaching along this line has been withheld. So little has this subject been understood that many persons have stoutly maintained that a Christian could never experience demon possession; but an ounce of fact is worth a pound of theory. Many Christians have been conscious of the working of evil spirits in some part of the being, and this manipulation continued until they were delivered as were those cases recorded in the New Testament.

Vital reckoning upon identification with a Crucified, Risen, Ascended, Glorified Lord, and *unceasing praise,* will keep the believer safe from the subtle working of the demons who are swarming about us.

There are times when the spoken word must be used, especially by those who are seeking to deliver bound souls, or in the times of special pressure that come to all Christians. The following words have been used by many and the results of their use prove their value: *"I refuse everything that is of the defeated one. I yield to everything that is of God, and I put the Blood of the Lord Jesus Christ, shed at Calvary, between me and all the powers of the defeated enemy."* Until one has spoken these words *aloud*, the results cannot be understood. We must remember that the spoken word carries weight in the invisible world. The powers of darkness cannot see what is down deep in our spirit. We cannot know ourselves what is taking place there, until God reveals it to us through our spiritual and mental perception—but the invisible intelligences hear our words and they watch our faces and note our acts. How necessary, then, that our words always state the facts as recorded in God's Written Word, and our faces reveal the peace and joy that come from believing, and our daily steps be ordered in His Word. We should never utter or write a discouraging word. Even a despondent, "Oh dear!" may betray the loophole that the watching powers of darkness will be quick to see.

THE ATTITUDE OF PRAISE

This matter of praising God is far more important than most Christians realize. There is a reason underlying the repeated *command,* "Praise ye the Lord." God knows what praise will do for His children; therefore not once, but many, many times, He bids them utter the words of praise. If a word of discouragement opens the door for the enemy, then a word of praise closes the door and locks it. Moreover, it drives the enemy far away. Nothing is more distasteful to evil spirits than the praise of a trustful child of God, and nothing more truly glorifies God than the sacrifice of praise.

On the wings of praise there will come into our hearts

and lives every desirable emotion, overflowing outpourings of God. It is not our love or our praise but God's own praise. Obey God who commands, "Praise ye the Lord."...But one may say, "Can I praise God when I do not feel like it?" Yes, praise Him because that is His will concerning you (1 Thes. 5:18) and He will meet and take care of the feeling. (Edgar K. Sellew)

God has commanded His people to praise Him, and certain conditions will not be realized until *all* obey. (See Psa. 67:5-6.)

Viewed from the psychological and physiological standpoints, the value of praise can scarcely be estimated, as it is impossible to tabulate all the beneficial results to be realized in the spiritual, mental and physical realm as this command is obeyed. What would be the result if Christians should begin to praise God continually? Surely great deliverance would be realized throughout the earth, and angels would see the clearing of the heavens as the reverberation of the praises of God's people mounted upward, and God would be glorified. Yet the average Christian considers literal obedience to the oft repeated command, "Praise ye the Lord," as foolish and fanatical, choosing instead to praise Him only when he *feels* like doing so.

TRANSFORMATION CONSIDERED PSYCHOLOGICALLY

The subject of Transformation may now be considered psychologically. The teacher should have the class read Romans 12:1-2. Verse 1 speaks of that complete dedication of the whole being which has already been described; the yielded *body,* manifesting the yielded powers of soul and spirit. Verse 2 describes the actual process of transformation as a *renewing of the mind.* That this expression may be the better understood, the relation of the mind or intellectual faculties to the other powers of the tripartite being of man should be explained.

With the powers of spirit we know God and our relation to Him and our relation morally to every object of creation. God's communications to man are in the form of intuitions, i.e., direct knowledge apart from the exercise of the intellectual faculties; but the mind has to deal with these intuitions of the spirit before they can be acted upon. The mind has also to deal with the claims of the affections and emotions and the record of the bodily senses; therefore we perceive its importance.

In the Garden of Eden we find Satan assailing the mind of Eve. He sought to substitute his lie for the intuitive knowledge of God's will which she had in her spirit and which her mind had attentively considered up to this time. He caused her mind to revolve around the possibilities that inhered in the choice to become "as (equal to) God," until with mental powers completely dazzled by the wonderful prospect, she used her power of choice—and the fatal deed was done.

We read in Proverbs 20:27 that "the spirit of man is the candle of the Lord," and it is this candle that is lighted by God the Holy Spirit at regeneration. We have seen that the new Life of God in Christ Jesus enters the spirit of man at the instant of regeneration and is intended to permeate the whole being, but this is accomplished only through the renewed mind. If the Christian refuses to present his entire being to God for renewal, then the unrenewed mind deals with the intuitions of the spirit, and the result is disastrous to Christian development and transformation. Many Christians refuse to yield their minds to God, yet think that they are able to understand the deep things of God. They talk about Eternal truths, they preach about them, they write books about them, yet they fail to understand them or lead others to understand them; for the things of God are spiritually discerned, and their thinking is performed by the *natural* mind. This is the solution of the otherwise unsolved problem as to the present day teaching of many persons whom we do not doubt are truly "born from above." Of course those persons who have not been regenerated have not even a renewed *spirit*. They are not able to understand anything that pertains to the Christian life. All that they say in regard to God and His Eternal Purpose is distinctly opposed to the Truth as stated in God's Written Word. Their teaching is not only unscriptural and blasphemous but it is illogical and puerile, betraying the darkness and weakness of an unrenewed personality.

The Christian who has said "the irrevocable, inclusive *yes*" to God, soon realizes and manifests a renewed condition of the mental powers. The mind becomes increasingly able to intelligently deal with the intuitions of the spirit. In other words, the mental life of the God-Man is manifested within the natural mind of the person, freeing it from the darkness and weakness resulting from sin, and also strengthening its natural powers.

The Apostle Paul was continually beseeching Christians to dedicate themselves wholly to God, because only so could they know that practical transformation whereby they would be able to "prove what is that good, and acceptable, and perfect will of God." (Notice the order and significance of these adjectives.) Without this transforming work of the Holy Spirit, they would to some extent become conformed to this world, i.e., to the great world system under the leadership of Satan, "the god of this world." (See 2 Cor. 4:4.)

"Conform" means "to shape in accordance with." For illustration: The metal worker pours hot metal into a mold and as it cools, it assumes the shape of the mold. The housekeeper pours fruit juice into a jelly mold and when it hardens, the jelly is in the shape of the mold. The metal and the fruit juice are conformed to their respective molds. It is very easy for Christians to be influenced by the great world system all about us. Unconsciously, Christians follow the ways of the world in matters of business and educational methods, social customs, dress, expenditures, recreation and conversation, while professing to follow Christ, and in many cases really desiring to put Him first. Christians are not to be conformed to this mold of Satan but to be conformed to God's mold, *the likeness of His Son* (Rom. 8:29), i.e., the glorified humanity of our Lord Jesus Christ.

Notice that the word *transform* indicates a change in the elemental substance, while "conform" denotes a change in form only. The metal is unchanged in substance when conformed to the mold. The jelly is precisely the same variety of fruit juice that was placed within the mold to harden. No real transformation has taken place; only conformation is realized.

No human being can become conformed to God's mold until there is a change from within, i.e., the introduction of a new life into the human personality. This new Life is for the purpose of permeating the entire personality, until transformation shall have resulted in complete conformation. The teacher should have the class read 2 Corinthians 3:18, R.V., also the Rotherham and Weymouth translations, if possible. Notice that this transforming work of the "Spirit of the Lord" is by degrees (from one degree of glory to another).

REFLECTING WHAT WE BEHOLD

The teacher should also call attention to the figure of the mirror employed here. A mirror can reflect only what it beholds; even so the Christian will reflect in his daily life only so much of Christ as he sees. If there is a veil upon his face, he will see imperfectly; therefore, he must so yield to God that the veil shall be taken away. Call attention to the veil upon the heart and the blinded minds mentioned in this chapter as true of unbelieving Israelites, and note the contrast in reference to the people of God. "We all with *unveiled* faces" see *Him*. But, do we see Him as clearly as we should? Does it not seem as if a veil was upon the minds of many Christians? They seem to be living in a sad twilight, reflecting an incomplete Christ, when it is their privilege to constantly gaze upon the glorious beauty of a Majestic Conqueror and to reflect Him in their lives.

Let us remember that as mirrors we cannot reflect what we do not see. If we see Christ in His Substitutionary work only, we shall not be able to manifest His Victory over sin and Satan; or, in other words, if we do not see Him as our Representative in every respect, the Holy Spirit will not be able to cause a manifestation of His Life in our daily lives. And how are we to see Him? By finding out what God's Written Word says about Him and believing every word that we read.

Conformity, the end; transformation, the way. From glory to glory up towards conformity; we are transformed into the same Image, from glory to glory. Step after step, out of the shame of self-complaint, into the glory of the Lamb-life, from glory to glory, even into the same Image....When a man awakens to the consciousness that he has not only been pardoned, but that he has by His Heavenly Father been foreordained to such a thing as conformity to the Image of the Son of God, everything loses its importance, its weight, its power. Joy cannot lift us up too high, and grief cannot break us down. Every circumstance brings us out of the wicked image of the First Adam, out of our wicked character into the full Image of the Son of God. (Pastor Stockmayer, in *Sanctified Ones*)

RESTFUL COOPERATION WITH THE HOLY SPIRIT

The teacher must so present every phase of the subject of transformation, that the members of the class will be led into a state of *restful cooperation* with the Holy Spirit. They must see that God, the Holy Spirit, will not fail to cause the yielded personality to appropriate all that God in Christ purchased at Calvary. The attitude of the Christian, which should be maintained day by day, is indicated in the following words:

Let us henceforth consider the Cross of Christ as a knife in the hands of the Holy Spirit to slay our sin-stained self life. And let us regard the Resurrected and Ascended Life of our Glorified Lord as an inexhaustible Storehouse from which the Holy Spirit supplies us with what we need for spirit, soul and body moment by moment.

The members of the class who have carefully followed the lessons up to this point will not be inclined to limit the "gospel" to the substitutionary work of Christ, precious as that is. They will hence-forth be able to perceive the full gospel message, to believe it, and earnestly desire to live it out and to tell it out.

In this course of study the attempt has been made to present the complete cycle of Redemptive truth and to show the correlation of subjects as plainly as possible.

It is hoped that the students following this method of Bible Study will be enabled to discover the scarlet thread of God's Plan of Redemption throughout the whole Book, and will perceive the relation of this Redemptive Plan to God's Eternal Purpose for the human race.

As a supplementary course in Redemption Studies, the books of Exodus, Leviticus, Numbers, Deuteronomy and Joshua in the Old Testament, and Hebrews in the New Testament, may be studied with great profit. Every detail of God's Plan of Redemption will be found pictured within these books and set forth in logical order. Redemption, in type, however, should not be presented to a class until the doctrinal truths as stated in God's Word are plainly perceived. It is also urged that the student carefully examine the epistles to ascertain what is therein stated in reference to the various subjects that have been presented in this course; e.g., notice what the Apostle Paul states in reference to the gospel which he preached in 1 Corinthians 15:1-4; Hebrews 10:12-17; 9:28. This may be summarized as follows: Christ died for our sins. He was buried. He rose again. He ascended to the right hand of God. He is coming again. These vital truths are stated again and again throughout the New Testament. Notice also that these statements are always shown to be "according to the Scriptures." The wonderful unity of God's Written Word is herein shown. Historical events that are narrated in the New Testament were predicted by writers of the Old Testament centuries before their fulfillment. Every detail of the historical execution of God's Plan of Redemption was typified in various ways, thousands of years before the Cross of Calvary.

BRIEF SUMMARY OF LESSONS STUDIED

It may be well for the members of the class to memorize the following sentences as a concise summary of the lessons studied:

Christ *died* that the sin-question of the human race might be settled in such a manner that God could consistently bestow sonship upon any one who should choose to receive the same.

He was *buried* that the termination of the old Adamic life might be plainly perceived.

He *arose* that the human race might have a new Federal Head (the Last Adam).

He *ascended* that His dominion might be manifested throughout the universe.

THE UNITY OF BELIEVERS

Having considered those conditions which made Redemption necessary, the execution of God's Plan of Redemption at Calvary, and the crises and results of appropriation, we now approach a subject, which if not as vital as those previously considered, is nevertheless of great importance to the earnest Christian. This is the Unity of believers, i.e., those who have appropriated the Life of God in Christ Jesus.

Biologically, the unity of beings upon a given plane of life is clearly seen; e.g., there are characteristic elemental qualities pertaining to animal life that are not found upon the plane of vegetable life. These qualities, inhering in all animals, serve to unify the entire animal creation, notwithstanding the great variety in family and the marked differences in the manifestation of this life.

Also upon the plane of human life, an inherent essential unity is seen. The Apostle Paul gave expression to this biological truth when he declared to the Athenians that God had "made of *one blood* all nations of men to dwell on all the face of the earth" (Acts 17:26).

If this essential unity is true of life in each of the lower planes, should we not naturally expect to find the same inherent principle on the highest plane—that of regenerated human life? That this unity exists, God's Word plainly declares; for we read in Ephesians 4:4-6, "There is one body, and one Spirit, even as ye have been called in one hope of your calling. One Lord, one faith, one baptism. One God and Father of all, who is above all and through all and in all." It was the manifestation of this unity for which Christ prayed in that marvelous prayer recorded in John 17, "I in them, and Thou in Me, that they may be perfected into one—and the glory which Thou gavest Me I have given them; that they may be one, as we are one."

This passage in Ephesians proves that all believers of every age and dispensation share the Life of God in Christ Jesus; i.e., they have Eternal or Uncreated Life, and this Life is the basis of their unity.

They are also saved in precisely the same manner—"By grace are ye saved through faith" (Eph. 2:8); and they are all to be glorified (see Rom. 8:30): "Whom He justified, them He also glorified." This unity, however, does not mean uniformity; for even as differences are observed in the manifestation of life on lower planes, so life upon this plane, even when conformed to Type, will not produce uniformity. Even as "one star differeth from another star in glory," so will the redeemed saints differ one from another in their glorified life.

Therefore, bearing in mind the difference between unity and uniformity, let us proceed to study another passage that preciously sets forth the oneness of believers.

ORGANIC UNITY OF THE BODY OF CHRIST

In 1 Corinthians 12:12 we read, "As the body is one and hath many members and all the members of that one body being many, are one body—so also is *the* Christ." Notice that this expression—"*the* Christ"—does not refer to Christ in His personality, but to Christ as completed by His members—the *Composite Christ*. Here we have an organic unity, of which Christ, in His personality, is the head (see Eph. 4:15), and all those who are joined to Him in Spirit and share His Life are members. Following the analogy of the human body, which is an organic unity because of the life-blood flowing through each and every member, we reason that every human being sharing Eternal Life must be a member of this Organic Unity—*the* Christ.

Whatever may be the dispensational teaching in reference to the Body of Christ, *organically this Body must include every regenerated human being.*

The same blood that is in the head of the human body—the physical, mortal body, flows through each member of the body even to the extremities. Therefore, most absurd would it be to say that a bit of flesh, through which the life-blood is flowing, is not a part of the body; for the members are unified by a common life-blood. Even so, the Life of God in Christ Jesus, unifies all members of the mystical Body of Christ. Therefore a human being, sharing His Life, must be a member of this Body of which He is the exalted Head, no matter in which dispensation he may have chosen to receive that Life.

WHAT IS MEANT BY DISPENSATION

At this point it will be well to explain what is meant by dispensation. Concerning this word, Dr. Farr says,

> The word "Dispensation" is rarely used as the designation of an epoch of time. It implies a method of working, an economy. It often implies time and then may be used as synonymous with age. There are seven dispensations: "The Paradisaic, Antediluvian, Patriarchal, Mosaic, Messianic, Christian and Millennial."

To put it very simply, the seven different dispensations are seven different methods employed by God, the Holy Spirit, in revealing vital truths to man. But here again, we must note the unity in diversity, or dispensational teaching will tend to confuse rather than to enlighten. Although the methods differ, the truths revealed are common to all the dispensations, as we shall see if we carefully examine the specific revelation of each dispensation. Reducing these revelations to their last analysis, we find that the truths revealed are those concerning God's Eternal Purpose for the human race, i.e., Sonship through faith in the Eternal Son.

In each dispensation, human beings could truthfully say, "God hath given us Eternal Life, and this Life is in His Son. He that hath the Son hath the Life, and he that hath not the Son, hath not the Life."

In the Paradisaic dispensation we see this Life symbolized by the tree of life in the midst of the garden, of which man might have partaken had he chosen so to do. This was God's first method of teaching human beings, but man's disobedience to the revealed will of God necessitated another method of teaching; therefore we see the "slain lamb," and perceive that identification with the sin-bearer was now the revelation of God to sinful man.

From this time we see God's wonderful Plan of Redemption, like the petals of the rose, slowly unfolding from dispensation to dispensation with increasing fragrance into the full blown flower. We see that each succeeding dispensation has served to reveal with increasing clearness the exceeding sinfulness of sin and the completeness of the marvelous Plan of Redemption that God's Love has provided. In each dispensation, man has become a child of God only through a definite act of faith. Each regenerated being has said, *"I am a sinner—saved by grace."*

Thus we see the unification of the dispensations, and we are able to perceive that dispensations and ages serve only as the temporary scaffolding of God's Eternal Structure. We may also liken the dispensations to the furrows in a cornfield. Until the harvest time, the corn growing in one furrow may be distinguished from that growing in another furrow; but when all the corn is stored in the corn bin, it is impossible to state in which furrow each ear grew. Therefore, we must be very careful not to unduly magnify dispensational methods and the diversities that are clearly discernible in the out-working of God's great Redemptive Plan. "The diversities are great—the unity is greater" (Adolph Saphir). Eventually only two classes of human beings will be found in the universe—those who share the Eternal Life of God and those who do not.

TOTALITY OF BELIEVERS NEEDED
TO COMPLETE THIS ORGANIC UNITY

The teacher should now call attention to the smaller circle attached to the large gilt disc symbolizing Uncreated Life, and explain that this circle symbolizes the totality of the regenerated human beings, i.e., the complete number of human personalities filled with the Uncreated or Eternal Life of God in Christ Jesus. We may also consider these saints as *God's Household*—His great family of "sons brought to glory"; and as each member of this Household is individually joined to Christ, we are led to see that these saints constitute the Body, of which He is the Head.

Following the analogy of the formation of the physical human body, we are able to see that the formation of this mystical Body is a hidden secret process. The language of Psalm 139:16, in reference to the literal physical human body, may well be applied to this mystical Body: "Thine eyes did see my substance, yet being unperfect, and in Thy book all my members were written, which in continuance were fashioned, when as yet there was none of them."

The Eternal Son needed a human, physical body for His great Sacrificial work and declares, "A body hast Thou prepared Me" (Heb. 10:5). As truly does He need a Body for the manifestation of that Redemptive work, and of this Body He can also say, "A Body hast Thou prepared Me"; and God has written in His Book all the members of this Body, "which in continuance were fashioned, when as yet there was none of them"; for we read in Revelation 13:8 and 17:8 of the names in the Book of the Life of the slain Lamb, *written from the foundation of the world.* We also read in Ephesians 1:4 that these members were chosen *"in Him before* the foundation of the world."

As a body is for the manifestation of that which is invisible, it follows that only the total number of regenerated human beings will adequately, completely manifest that measure of Eternal Life which God has stored in His Eternal Son for human beings. It will take *all* the saints of every age and dispensation to embody this Life, and not until the last being who was "marked out before the foundation of the world" has appropriated and manifested this Life, can the mystical Body of Christ organically be complete.

Christ's prayer "that they all may be one in Us" will yet be fully answered, and

> All His saints from all the ages,
>   Every clime and tongue
> All together then will worship
>   In a faultless song.

Thus we see that in a time yet future, Christ shall "see of the travail of His soul and be *satisfied."*

ALL SAINTS SAVED
BY GRACE THROUGH FAITH

The teacher should again call attention to the fact that each member of this great company of the glorified redeemed has been saved by "grace through faith." It matters not in which age or dispensation grace was appropriated—all alike sing praise to the Lamb whose Blood has washed them from their sins.

The saints of the Old Testament, as well as the saints of the New, put faith in the Lamb of Calvary and received Eternal Life thereby. This fact is brought out very clearly in Hebrews 11, which should now be carefully read. The nature of faith also may be perceived as we study this chapter. *Faith is believing God's Word to the extent of acting upon it.* Notice that every person mentioned here *acted upon God's Word.* "By faith Abel offered unto God a more excellent sacrifice than Cain, by which he obtained the testimony that he was righteous, God testifying of his gifts; and by it he being dead, yet speaketh." "By faith Enoch was translated that he should not see death; and was not found, because God had translated him; for before his translation he had the testimony, that he pleased God." Are these men behind the New Testament saints or the saints of the present time? Is their "testimony" inferior to ours? Surely not. Rather are they far in advance of the majority of Christians.

Think of Enoch, the seventh from Adam, prophesying of the Coming of the Lord "with tens of thousands of His saints to execute judgment upon all, and to convict all that are ungodly among them of all their ungodly deeds which in their ungodliness they have committed, and of all the hard things which ungodly sinners have spoken against Him." (See Jude 14-15.) Who taught him that evil men would "wax worse and worse, deceiving and being deceived" (see 2 Tim. 3:13), and that instead of growing better as the appearing of Christ drew near, the world would become increasingly wicked and ungodly? It was the same Holy Spirit who revealed these things to Paul, Who shows them to us, and concerning Whom, Christ said before His Ascension, "He will show you things to come." And if the Holy Spirit revealed to Enoch the Coming of Christ *with* His saints to judge the world, did He not as plainly reveal the fact of His Coming *for* His saints—His ready, watching ones—to take them out of the ungodly world conditions before the terrible Tribulation period; and did he not live in the light of His Coming? Surely Enoch, in the Antediluvian dispensation, was not behind those watching saints who today are seeking to have the testimony that they please God before they are ready for translation. Intervening years make no difference whatever; the Enochs are one in spirit, in walk, in objective.

The list of the heroes of faith is a long one, but it is not complete. Many, many others whose names are not written obtained "a good testimony through faith." Were each one to be questioned as to his relation to God, he would reply, "I am a sinner saved by grace, through faith; therefore a child of God." Dispensational exteriors seem to place the Old Testament saints in a far away period, but their confession of faith and the fact that they share with us Uncreated (Eternal) Life, that has *no past*—brings them near; and we *feel the oneness.*

Abel's name appears first upon this Faith Roll, but was he the first human being to put faith in God's Slain Lamb? Bearing in mind our definition of faith, which is "believing God's Word to the extent of acting upon it," let us look a little farther back, before the birth of Abel.

In another section of these studies, attention has been called to the attitude of Adam and Eve in relation to the slain lamb whose blood was shed that they might be clothed, and the statement was made that through the illumination of God the Holy Spirit, Adam and Eve understood enough of God's Plan of Redemption to put faith in God's Slain Lamb. The proof of that statement we now find in Genesis 3:20 and 4:1. Adam believed God's word concerning "the seed of the woman," who should crush the head of Satan; therefore he *immediately acted his faith* by calling his wife Eve, which signifies that not only was she to become the mother of all living, the mother of the human race, but it was the expression of his confident expectation of the Coming One, of whom God had spoken. This confident attitude of faith was shared by Eve, who exclaims upon the birth of Cain, "I have gotten a Man—even Yahweh" (Gen. 4:1, Rotherham).

Concerning this subject we will quote from an exceedingly helpful book, *Yahveh Christ—The Memorial Name:*

> The exclamation of Eve at the birth of Cain may be expressed with more faithfulness as to the original by the

rendering, "I have received Him, even *He who is to come.*"
The ancient root form, Havah, from which comes Yahveh,
gave rise, through the idea of "breathing," its original *"sense
idea,"* to the two Hebrew verbs "to be" and "to desire." From
"to breathe," as the sign of existence, was derived "to be";
and from "to breathe or *pant after"* came "to long for," "to
desire." How doubly significant in this view is the exclama-
tion of Eve: "I have received Him, even He who will be."
"The Promised One." "The Longed for."

Although they were disappointed to find that Cain was not the
"Promised One," yet they did not lose faith in God's word, as the
name given to their third son, Seth, plainly implies (see Gen. 4:25);
and from the seed of Seth descended Mary, *the woman,* whose *seed,*
Jesus, was the object of the faith of Adam and Eve. Their names are
not mentioned in Hebrews 11 for obvious reasons. They were the
parents of the human race. Their *sin* affected each human being
because of the law of heredity. Their *faith* was an *individual* matter
and would have no bearing upon the status of the human race.
Adam was the first Representative man; therefore, it was essential
that only such of his acts as were representative in character
should be plainly set forth in God's Written Word. His faith was an
individual act affecting only himself. It was not representative in
character, as is plainly shown in the fact that Cain, his firstborn,
was the first human being who refused to put faith in God's Slain
Lamb.

THE MARRIAGE SUPPER OF THE LAMB

Having considered the organic unity of believers as indicated
by the figure of the "Body of Christ," let us now consider their
unity from the standpoint of love and devotedness. In connection
with this subject another figure is employed by the Holy Spirit.
We find its most complete mention in Revelation 19:7 and
21:9-27. In these passages, the figure of a marriage ceremony is
used, to convey most precious truths concerning the relation of the
regenerated ones to the Lord and also to one another.

A marriage, in its true sense, implies the union of two beings upon the same plane of life, whose hearts are indissolubly linked in the bonds of undying love. This marriage is between Christ, the Lamb, and glorified believers. The words, "His wife hath made herself ready," seem to imply that the marriage ceremony depends upon her preparedness. Alas, that the Lamb has been kept waiting so long for His Bride to make herself ready! Some of those constituting this Composite Bride will make ready only when the Tribulation period destroys their earthly perspective.

We read in Revelation 7:9 that during the short but dreadful Tribulation period, "a great multitude which no *man* could number," but whose names were written in the book of the Life of the Lamb from the foundation of the world, suddenly perceive God's glorious Plan of Redemption in its full-robed splendor and quickly appropriate all that they behold, and are taken out of the more terrible tribulation woes, and stand before the throne and before the Lamb, clothed with white robes and palms (the symbol of victory) in their hands, and they join in the song of the redeemed who have preceded them. Nowhere in the whole Bible is the tender, unutterable Love of God more blessedly shown than in this passage. Read it carefully, and note every word that is used in reference to this great company of *tribulation overcomers;* for perhaps some for whom we are now praying will be there.

Says Mr. Mead in his most helpful exposition of the Apocalypse,

> It is significant that this most glorious event (the Marriage Supper of the Lamb) is placed by the inspiring Spirit of truth just here (in chapter 19), and not in chapter 4 or 5; for there is where it would seem necessary to assign it a place if they are right who hold that the Church of God, the Bride of Christ, is wholly removed, once and for all, from the world before the time spoken of in the vision of chapter 4. By these it is affirmed that the saints and martyrs made during the Tribulation are not members of the Body of Christ,

that they belong to another order of redeemed ones. Not only do we find nothing in the whole Word of God to favor of this view, but many things have been pointed out in the course of this study which indicate that *all those who are saved during the entire Tribulation period* are also "fellow members of the Body," which is the Church of Christ, the "Church of the Firstborn." And now, as a further and most conclusive witness to the same, is the passage we are now considering; for it is not till the last saint shall have been caught up in the rapture of the gleaning time, that the Announcement is made that "His wife hath made herself ready."

The teacher should deal as simply and logically with the subject of "the Bride of Christ" as has already been done with the subject of the Body of Christ. "The Body speaks of oneness in *life* and *nature;* the Bride, of union in mutual *love* and *devotion.* There is no contradiction whatever" (Max I. Reich).

HOW A BELIEVER BECOMES A MEMBER OF THE BRIDE

We have already seen that one becomes a member of the Body of Christ the instant he accepts the Life of Christ. He enters into that deep, loving heart union with Him which indicates the attitude of the Bride, when he says the "irrevocable, inclusive *yes*" to Him. Love is more than emotion. The test of love is not what one *feels,* but what he will *do* for another. Therefore, before the Marriage Supper of the Lamb, each human being who is organically one with Him will have become one with Him in love and devotion. Furthermore, each saint will be glorified before the marriage takes place; i.e., the created human personality of each will have been filled with the Uncreated Life of God; even the earthy bodies will have partaken of Immortality. Note that the individual personality is *not destroyed,* but emptied of sin and filled with Eternal Life.

The "Supper" indicates the rejoicing over the realization of this long looked for, ardently desired consummation. Words fail to describe the beauty of this Bride of the Lamb as she stands by His side radiant with the "glory of God."

> And He shall lead His Bride, His Joy and Care,
>> With blissful singing to His Father's throne.
> With eyes undimmed shall she her God behold,
>> Behold Him face to face, and walk by sight,
> Not trusting only, as in days of old,
>> But seeing with her eyes Eternal Light.
> The great Salvation mystery shall unfold
>> In that high vision of Love infinite.

THE GREAT HARLOT – THE ANTITHESIS OF THE BRIDE OF THE LAMB

The attention of the Bible student should now be directed to the next event in connection with the manifestation of Christ's Redemptive work.

During the tribulation period the world has passed through a series of unparalleled woes, the climax of which was the destruction of the Great Harlot, the antithesis of the Bride of the Lamb. Under the figure of a city, called Babylon—from Babel—meaning *confusion,* we find the world system of Satan in its comprehensive character, portrayed in Revelation 17 and 18.

The student should not think of this "Babylon" as a literal city. To do so would be to miss the symbolism. That a literal city is not indicated is proven by several phrases, particularly verse 24 of chapter 18. Here we read that "in her was found the blood of prophets, and of *all* that had been slain upon the earth." This statement precludes the idea of the rebuilt city of literal Babylon. Besides, God had said that the literal city of Babylon should *never* be rebuilt. (See Isa. 13:20.) This direful prediction, however, does not apply to the *province* of Babylon or Babylonia. The province has not been without inhabitants since the fall of the city of Babylon, but the city proper remains to this day a heap of ruins concerning which one writer says, "More thorough destruction than that which has overtaken Babylon cannot well be conceived—even its site has been a subject of dispute." The noted scholar, John Urquhart, in his comparatively recent book, *The Wonders of Prophecy,* devotes several pages to the present conditions of the ruins of the city of Babylon as a literal fulfillment of the prophecy of Isaiah 13:20. Seiss speaks of this Satanic Bride-City as "the whole body of organized alienation from God." This phrase gives us the key to the interpretation of the whole passage, and we are enabled to see that the Holy Spirit is portraying in a figurative, graphic manner the city built by Satan, of human beings who have deliberately refused to put faith in God's Slain Lamb.

While the Marriage Supper of the Lamb is celebrated above, the Great Harlot meets her doom in the world below. In other words, the great world system of Satan comes to an end; and now Christ, with His glorified followers, returns to earth to "make His enemies the footstool of His feet" and to manifest His already existing but hitherto invisible *Kingdom* upon the earth.

EARTHLY DOMINION OF CHRIST
AND HIS FOLLOWERS

The whole groaning creation is now "delivered from the bondage of corruption into the glorious liberty of the children of God." (See Rom. 8:21.) The results of Adam's loss of dominion through sin have caused that unutterable "groaning" in the animal and vegetable creation that has been heard through the centuries. But now all is changed; for the Last Adam and His "seed," the host of the redeemed, now exercise dominion throughout the earth. Beasts no longer prey upon one another but return to their Edenic condition as described in Isaiah 11:6-9; 65:25. Thorns, briars, thistles, weeds, no longer encumber the ground; but vegetation once more rejoices in its normal, luxuriant beauty and fertility as created.

Those political, financial, social conditions, of which poets have dreamed, and concerning which statesmen and reformers have devoted much thought, are now realized, and the glorious

Millennial Age manifests, as no previous dispensation could do, the fruits of Christ's Redemptive Work at Calvary. The teacher should call attention to such passages as describe the ideal conditions of this blessed time when

> His blessings flow
> Far as the curse is found,

e.g., Isaiah 11:4-9; 35; 65:21-25; Micah 4:1-4.

THE NEW HEAVEN AND NEW EARTH

However, glorious as is the Millennial Age, it will not prove to be the final manifestation of the results of Christ's Redemptive Work. Not only has sin ruined the human race and wrought great changes in the animal and vegetable creation, but it has left great scars in the earth itself.

We have previously considered the chaotic condition of this planet which was the result of Satan's sin, and we need to remember that the sin of man has brought about great topographical and meteorological changes upon our globe and conditions that again call for God's work of reconstruction.

While it may not be wise to dwell upon this subject, yet the attention of the student may be directed to 2 Peter 3:5-13, where the analogy is shown between the watery baptism of "the world that then was," and the fiery baptism that awaits the *world that now is.*

There are not wanting intimations of a conflagration of this kind, as students of natural science well know; and it has seemed as if this catastrophe were held back only by miraculous intervention. We know, however, that it cannot take place until after the Millennium, when God's time will have arrived for the complete purging of this earth from every trace of sin. That the earth will not be destroyed, we know from God's own declarations as found in Psalm 104:5; 119:90; Ecclesiastes 1:4, and other passages, and because we read of *Nations upon the earth* after this event has taken place. (See Rev. 21:24-26.)

Whatever new cataclysms or disasters are yet to befall this planet, we are assured that they will not be as disastrous even as Noah's flood; for God covenanted then, and said: "I will not *again* curse the ground any more for man's sake, neither will I *again* smite any more every living thing as I have done" (Gen. 8:21-22). (from *Lectures on the Apocalypse,* by Seiss)

Note: If the student will carefully read the article on "Theory of the Deluge," by Dr. A. T. Pierson in *Many Infallible Proofs,* this statement will be better understood and appreciated.

How God will care for the earthly creation during this time of the dissolving (or loosing) of the elements, we do not know; but He has promised to do so and He will.

In Revelation 21 we read of a new (or renewed) heaven and earth; and now we are permitted to gaze upon the final manifestation of God's redeemed children, as shown upon the last page of the Written Word.

As the Great Harlot, "drunken with the blood of the saints and martyrs of Jesus" (Rev. 17:5-6), was first shown us to reveal the character of "Babylon," which is to be regarded as "organized alienation from God," and then Babylon, the city, as this organized alienation in its complete and final manifestation, so the wife of the Lamb in her spotless robes and radiant beauty was first shown to reveal the love and devotion of the body of believers, and now the "Holy City" reveals the unification of believers in its organized and final manifestation.

THE HOLY CITY – THE BRIDE OF THE LAMB

Here is a city of God, and it is at the same time a city of man. No reader thinks for a moment that it is literally described here in the dimensions of equal length and breadth and height. This is a figurative description, meant to convey spiritual conceptions....It is curiously described as though it were built of *men*. It is a community....This city, built of redeemed men, is open to all men, but only such as have an affinity for God will go in. It is also a Bridal City. The New Jerusalem is the Bride of the Lamb, and those who do not belong to the Lamb as a wife belongs to her husband, by the sacred espousal of faith and love, will never have, nor desire to have, a part in this City of God. (Dr. A. T. Pierson, in *The Bible and Spiritual Criticism*)

As the "holy temple" described in Ephesians 2:19-22 was built of "living stones," so this glorious city is built of redeemed, glorified human beings. And here we see the diversity as well as unity. The buildings in a literal city are not uniform in size. Some are large and some are small; so in this city, some dwellings are of large dimensions and some are very small comparatively; but all alike partake of the glory of God and shine with light most precious, clear as crystal. We can think of the Apostles Paul, Peter and John as towering buildings compared with many saints, and we picture Enoch, Elijah and other Old Testament saints as structures of large dimensions; yet in all this City there is no dwelling that is lacking in perfect, finished proportions.

Best of all, this City is the habitation of God. In the beginning of our studies we noted several passages in which there was a strange blending of two figures, the architectural and the parental. Here we see them again in their complete unfolding. Here is a City "marked out" before the founding of the world, "whose Architect and Builder is God"; and here is the vast host of redeemed, glorified human beings whom He can clasp in His Arms and call *His glorified sons*. "Behold the tabernacle of God is with men, and *He will dwell in them* and they shall be *His people*" (Rev. 21:3).

And now Christ can "see of the travail of His soul and be satisfied"; for the curse is removed, and His redeemed ones see His face, and His Name (meaning His Nature) is written on their foreheads, and they serve Him forever more.

Now we see the Paradise of God, of which the Edenic Paradise was a type; and here is "the river of water of life bright as crystal, proceeding out of the throne of God and of the Lamb"; and here also is the Tree of Life; not the literal tree of Eden, but that which the literal tree symbolized. No longer is it guarded by Cherubim and the revolving sword-flame, for Calvary's Sacrifice has opened the way forever. It is interesting to observe that the Greek word used here (Rev. 22:2, 14) is not *dendron,* which is used to designate the literal tree of vegetable growth, but *xylon,* which denotes something made from the tree—literally *timber* or *beam.* It is the same word that is used in Galatians 3:13 [and] therefore suggests the Cross of Calvary. Very significant, then, is its use in this passage, for it reveals the fact that to sinful human beings, partaking of the fruit of the Tree of Life means the appropriation of all the Redemptive Work of Calvary. In other words, it speaks of identification with God's Slain Lamb in His Death and Resurrection. And may not the expression "the *leaves* of the tree were for the healing of the nations," refer to the beneficent results of the general appropriation of the fruits of Redemption in that happy time, as manifested in the absence of the selfishness, jealousy, hatred and strife that characterize the nations at the present time?

The created right to the Tree of Life was forfeited through sin, but those who have washed their robes in the Blood of the Lamb now have the Redemptive right to freely eat of the Tree of Life, and thus enter through the gates into the City. And the gates are not closed. They remain invitingly open; thus showing us that even to the *age of the ages,* Christ's Redemptive Work at Calvary may be appropriated by whomsoever will take the Life of the Lamb.

THE ATTITUDE OF THE CHRISTIAN

We have traced the appropriation and manifestation of Redemption from age to age, and now let us consider what should be the attitude of the Christian in view of the wonderful revelation that God has given us.

There must be a constant recognition of our identification with our Crucified, Risen, Victorious, Ascended Lord, and definite reckoning upon His Life, moment by moment, if we are to demonstrate the completeness of His Redemptive work as fully as He desires, before He comes.

God the Holy Spirit is preparing a "little flock" to overcome even as He overcame. Christ would not wish to return until He could say of these overcoming ones, "They overcame by the Blood of the Lamb, and by the word of their testimony; and they loved not their lives unto the death." (See Rev. 12:11.)

Notice the promises to the overcomers, in the second and third chapters of The Revelation. *They mean something.*

Dogmatic assertion ill becomes a Christian who is looking for the Coming of Christ; therefore the teacher should not insist upon the acceptance of any particular view as to those who are translated in the First Rapture. Possibly a more careful study of the Oriental harvest time and the various offerings connected therewith, would revolutionize many theories that are advanced at the present time.

The main question to be considered is *individual preparedness* and a walk with God like Enoch of old. The Christian should remember that the Life of the God-Man is for each member of His Body, moment by moment.

Simply and continuously should the Christian live out the "Life of the Man in the Glory." It is not a hard, strained life; rather it is the *normal* life of a Christian. We are the channels through which His Life flows to others, refreshing us meanwhile.

It is a blessed life, because we realize our need and utter dependence; consequently we are kept from self-energy and self-esteem.

Every moment of every day, we may draw from His fullness for all our needs.

Continually may we sing:

> There's a Man in the Glory
>   Whose Life is for me.
> He's pure and He's holy,
>   Triumphant and free.
> He's wise and He's loving,
>   Tender is He;
> And His Life in the Glory,
>   My life must be.
>
> There's a Man in the Glory
>   Whose Life is for me.
> He overcame Satan;
>   From bondage He's free.
> In Life He is reigning;
>   Kingly is He;
> And His Life in the Glory,
>   My life must be.
>
> There's a Man in the Glory
>   Whose Life is for me.
> In Him is no sickness;
>   No weakness has He.
> He's strong and in vigor
>   Buoyant is He;
> And His Life in the Glory
>   My life may be.
>
> There's a Man in the Glory
>   Whose Life is for me.
> His peace is abiding;
>   Patient is He.
> He's joyful and radiant,
>   Expecting to see
> His Life in the Glory
>   Lived out in me.